Fig. 1: Naramata and the south Okanagan from the KVR.

Okanagan Country

An Outdoor Recreation Guide

by

Murphy Shewchuk

SONOTEK® PUBLISHING LTD.
P.O. Box 1752
Merritt, B.C. Canada V0K 2B0

3

Canadian Cataloguing in Publication Data

Shewchuk, Murphy.
   Okanagan country

Includes bibliographical references and index.
ISBN 0-929069-04-8

   1. Outdoor recreation—British Columbia—Okanagan Valley—Guidebooks. 2. Okanagan Valley (B.C.) —History—Guidebooks. 3. Okanagan Valley (B.C.) —Guide-books. 4. Natural history—British Columbia —Okanagan Valley—Guide-books. I. Title.
GV191.46.B7853 1992   917.11'5   C92-091554-X

SONOTEK® PUBLISHING LTD.
P.O. Box 1752,
Merritt, B.C.
Canada V0K 2B0

Telephone (604) 378-5930

Book design by Murphy Shewchuk.
Photographs and maps by Murphy Shewchuk unless otherwise credited.

Distributed by Sandhill Book Marketing, #99 - 1270 Ellis Street (Rear), Kelowna, B.C. Canada V1Y 4E1   Telephone (604) 763-1406

Printed in Canada by Peerless Printers, Kamloops, B.C.

Dedication

To my parents
Julia & Murphy Shewchuk of Keremeos.

Acknowledgments

The history of the Okanagan Valley, gleaned from many published sources including the Okanagan Historical Society Reports, N.L. "Bill" Barlee's many books, and history books on Kelowna, Penticton, Vernon and the many smaller communities, have helped me to better understand the development of the Okanagan Valley. To list all these sources here would only repeat the bibliography that is at the back of the book, but I do wish to acknowledge their importance.

Displays in the museums throughout the valley have added a physical presence to the printed word. The staff at these museums have been particularly helpful. I would especially like to thank Randy Manuel of the Penticton Museum for his extraordinary efforts.

Others have also helped considerably. My wife Katharine and grand-daughter Bridget have traveled extensively with me, recording the images that we saw on paper and occasionally serving as subjects for my photographs. Nancy Wise, Jennifer Beckett and Gill Foss reviewed my manuscript and offered many constructive comments. Ches Lyons and the staff of Cathedral Lakes Lodge were extremely generous with their help, as were the staff at Headwaters Fishing Camp and Chute Lake Resort. Joan Burbridge and Mark Zuehlke of Kelowna; Clint Neilsen and Rick Howie of B.C. Parks; R.T (Bob) Gibbard of Naramata; Harley Hatfield, Victor Wilson and Bruce Morgenstern of Penticton all assisted with their knowledge and expertise. I must also thank Art Bailey, who volunteered considerable information about Fintry, on the west side of Okanagan Lake.

Murphy O. Shewchuk

•••

Preface

Bitish Columbia's beautiful Okanagan Valley, surrounded by majestic snow-capped mountains, has attracted visitors and residents for thousands of years. The Natives who lived here were "discovered" by the fur traders in the early 1800s. The 1860s brought the first settlers who soon learned that the land could produce fine fruit in abundance. Word of this Shangri-la along the lakes spread, attracting visitors from all parts of the world. Many stayed to enjoy the rich, relaxed lifestyle of the Okanagan Valley.

Okanagan Country is intended to be a guide to outdoor recreation in the Okanagan Valley and surrounding mountains with the general emphasis on individual or family activities. The geographical size and diversity of the Okanagan drainage basin lends itself to a great variety of activities, ranging from skiing, hiking and climbing in the mountains and upland plateau to boating, swimming and scuba diving in the many fine lakes of the Okanagan system. Climate variations also contribute to the diversity. Sheltered valleys and timbered mountain slopes present vastly different opportunities from the mid-elevation grasslands or the semi-desert bottomland. Each area has its appeal and its special season—and seasons often overlap. You can, for example, spend a beautiful spring morning skiing in the alpine glades and the afternoon lounging on a beach or photographing wildflowers on a hillside.

This book has been nearly two years in the research, writing and assembly stage with at least two decades of background research and travel. It quickly became apparent that it would be impossible for me to deal with the rapidly expanding golf scene in the Okanagan region. Alpine skiing has also seen considerable growth in recent years and continues to experience major changes, as resorts expand and alter their focus, due to growing customer demands and gradual climate changes. The skiing references here are intended to present my impressions at the time of my research.

It also became apparent that, even with these limitations, one book could not possibly cover every recreational opportunity, thus a second volume on the north Okanagan and Shuswap is being considered.

I believe, however, that you will find *Okanagan Country* to be a valuable resource when you feel the need for a quiet place to explore, hike, bike, fish, relax, or photograph nature.

•••

Table of Contents

1 **Central Okanagan: an Overview**   13
Kelowna and Surrounding Area

2 **Knox Mountain**   15
Hiking Trails in the Heart of Kelowna

3 **Woodhaven Nature Conservancy**   17
Kelowna's Best Kept Secret

4 **Bertram Creek Regional Park**   19
Pack your Picnic Basket

5 **Okanagan Mountain Park**   21
From Sagebrush to Huckleberries

6 **Chute Lake Loop**   27
Follow the Kettle Valley Line

7 **West Kettle Route—Highway 33**   33
Silver, Snow and the KVR

8 **McCulloch Road**   41
Backroad with a View

9 **Bear Creek Park**   45
Wild Canyons to Waterfront

10 **Last Mountain**   49
Ski Trails and Fishing Lakes

11 **Hardy Falls Park**   51
Peachland's Pleasant Getaway

12 **Headwaters Lakes**   55
Floating Islands and Fighting Trout

13 **Bear Road**   63
Upland Lakes and Mountain Backroads

14 **South Okanagan: An Overview**   69
Similkameen/South Okanagan/Boundary

Table of Contents

15 Okanagan Lake Park   71
Camping and more, by Okanagan Lake

16 Giant's Head Mountain   75
A Top with a View

17 Osprey Lakes Road   79
The Backroad to Princeton

18 Nickel Plate Road   83
Skiing, Fishing and a Gold Mine

19 Cathedral Provincial Park   91
Wilderness With Access

20 Fairview Road   99
A Grist Mill and a Gold Mine

21 White Lake Road   107
Listening to the Stars

22 Mount Baldy Loop   111
From Sand Dunes to Ski Slopes

23 Conkle Lake Loop   119
Backroad to an Upland Getaway

24 Haynes Point Park   125
A Sandspit in Osoyoos Lake

25 The Okanagan Desert   129
Osoyoos Oxbows & Haynes Ecological Reserve

26 North Okanagan: An Overview   133
Vernon and Area

27 Ellison Provincial Park   135
Rocky Headlands and Sheltered Coves

28 Kalamalka Lake Park   139
Rock Bluffs, Rattlesnakes and Beaches

29 Silver Star Park and Village   143
Winter Skiing and Summer Cycling

30 Westside Road   **147**
   Spallumcheen to Westbank

31 Mabel Lake Road (East Side)   **153**
   Lumby to Three Valley via Mabel Lake

32 The Mabel Lake Shortcut!   **161**
   Three Valley to Enderby via Mabel Lake.

33 Bibliography and Sources   **167**
   Selected Bibliography
   Maps
   Addresses

34 Index   **170**

35 About the Author   **176**

Maps

Map 1: Woodhaven Nature Conservancy area.   18

Map 2: Kelowna and Okanagan Mission area.   20

Map 3: Okanagan Mountain Park (Courtesy of B.C. Parks).   22

Map 4: Chute Lake Road and the Kettle Valley Railway.   29

Map 5: West Kettle Road (Highway 33).   34

Map 6: McCulloch Road and the Kettle Valley Railway.   43

Map 7: Bear Creek Park (Courtesy of B.C. Parks).   46

Map 8: Headwaters Lakes area.   59

Map 9: Sunset Lake to Kelowna.   64

Map 10: Giant's Head Park and downtown Summerland.   78

Map 11: Summerland to Princeton via Osprey Lake.   81

Map 12: Penticton -- Apex Alpine -- Hedley.   85

Map 13: Keremeos and Cathedral Park Area.   93

Map 14: Cawston to Oliver via Fairview Road.   103

Map 15: Oliver to Kaleden via White Lake Road.   108

Map 16: Oliver -- Mount Baldy -- Bridesville.   115

Map 17: Conkle Lake Provincial Park and area.   122

Map 18: Osoyoos and Haynes Point Park.   126

Map 19: Oliver to Osoyoos Lake.   132

Map 20: Ellison Provincial Park (Courtesy of B.C. Parks).   136

Map 21: Kalamalka Lake Provincial Park access routes.   141

Map 22: Westside Road.   149

Map 23: Enderby -- Mabel Lake -- Three Valley Area.   155

Photographs

Fig. 1: Naramata and the south Okanagan from the KVR.   2

Fig. 2: The "Sails" by R. Dow Reid (Bernard and Abbott).   14

Fig. 3: Nancy Wise and Joan Burbridge (L) at Woodhaven.   17

Fig. 4: Prickly-pear cactus in blossom.   24

Fig. 5: Divide Lake in Okanagan Mountain Park.   25

Fig. 6: Cyclists on the Bellevue Creek Trestle.   28

Fig. 7: Taking a break from skiing at Big White.   37

Fig. 8: Carmi School in September, 1984.   40

Fig. 9: Hikers on a bridge across Lambly (Bear) Creek.   48

Fig. 10: Jackpine Lake, near Westbank, B.C.   49

Fig. 11: Hardy Falls on Peachland (Deep) Creek.   53

Fig. 12: Sunset Lake, looking east.   56

Fig. 13: Fishermen at MacDonald Lake, west of Peachland.   57

Fig. 14: A mule deer doe near Headwaters Lake #1.   60

Fig. 15: Canoeing on Pennask Lake.   65

Fig. 16: Beach at Christie Memorial Park, Skaha Lake.   69

Table of Contents

Fig. 17: A robin eyes the photographer from a poplar.   72

Fig. 18: A nearly-deserted beach in the morning light.   73

Fig. 19: Summerland from Giant's Head Mountain.   76

Fig. 20: Sighting tubes help distinguish local landmarks.   77

Fig. 21: Fisherman and dog on Chain Lake.   80

Fig. 22: Cross country skiing in the high country.   86

Fig. 23: Glacier Lake in Cathedral Park.   95

Fig. 24: Giant Cleft in Cathedral Park.   97

Fig. 25: Pumpkin display at Barrington Market in Keremeos.   100

Fig. 26: Keremeos Grist Mill on Upper Bench Road.   101

Fig. 27: Arrowleaf balsamroot near Oliver.   105

Fig. 28: Dominion Radio Astrophysical Observatory.   109

Fig. 29: Catching a few rays on Mount Baldy.   112

Fig. 30: Mine tipple at Camp McKinney (Sept. 1985).   117

Fig. 31: Waterfalls in Conkle Lake Park.   121

Fig. 32: Ferreira's Fruit Market in East Osoyoos.   128

Fig. 33: Historic Haynes Ranch building at Road 22.   131

Fig. 34: Okanagan Lake and headlands at Ellison Park.   134

Fig. 35: Kalamalka Lake, from 10 km south of Vernon.   139

Fig. 36: A wary rattlesnake watches a wary photographer.   142

Fig. 37: Silver Star Village at night.   143

Fig. 38: A grouse hen in a sub-alpine meadow.   145

Fig. 39: Steel-wheel farm tractor at O'Keefe Ranch.   148

Fig. 40: Fairy Slipper (Calypso bulbosa) in the forest.   152

Fig. 41: Cascade Falls, east of Mabel Lake.   157

Fig. 42: Picking huckelberries near Wap Lake.   160

Fig. 43: Mabel Lake, from Noisy Creek recreation site.   165

Fig. 44: Murphy Shewchuk   176

11

Symbols used in this book.

 Photographic opportunities

 Swimming beach

 Backpacking and hiking trails

 Rock climbing or mountaineering

 Horse riding trails

 Cycle paths or trails

 Motorcycle trails or race tracks

 Backroads routes

 Angling and sport fishing

 Hunting and/or shooting sports

 Sailing or wind-surfing

 Boat launch site

 Marina

 Snowmobile trails

 Cross-country or Nordic ski trails

 Snow-shoe trails

 Downhill or alpine ski area

 Ski-jumping

 Picnic site

 Shelter

 Tent site or wilderness campground

 RV campground

 RV park or mixed campground

 RV sani-station

 Point of Interest

 Viewpoint

1

Central Okanagan: an Overview

Kelowna and Surrounding Area

Kelowna has grown at such a rapid pace in recent years that a newcomer may initially be impressed with its urban sprawl rather than the quiet places to be found with further exploring. Kelowna and the surrounding area offers many outdoor recreation opportunities if you take the time to look beyond (and sometimes between) its hotels, shopping centres and housing developments.

Knox Mountain Park, for example, can be quiet early in the morning—as long as it doesn't happen to be the May holiday weekend when the Knox Mountain Hill Climb is in full steam. Woodhaven Nature Conservancy, at the end of Raymer Road in Okanagan Mission can be quiet—or noisy—any day of the week. It depends on whether or not you consider the frantic chatter of a squirrel part of the quiet or part of the noise. The pathways in Mission Creek Park are seldom devoid of people, but it is easy to let the burble of the water flowing through the kokanee spawning channel carry you away from your surroundings.

The trails into the north slopes of Okanagan Mountain Provincial Park can also be quiet and devoid of people—even in mid-summer. Access to the park is off Lakeshore Road from Kelowna, by boat or via the Chute Lake Road, north of Naramata. In keeping with the wilderness nature of the park, facilities are minimal at all entry points.

Bear Creek Provincial Park, on the west shore of Okanagan Lake, has full facilities, but the spectacular canyon and waterfalls encourage wild birds and animals—and satisfy the need for free space that is part of the wild animal within all of us. Hardy Falls Park in Peachland has a canyon and waterfall, although at a much smaller scale. It is also much more accessible for those with limited mobility.

If you have that urge to get mobile, backroads lead up into the hills from Peachland, Westbank and Kelowna where you will often find places to golf, trek, cycle, fish or camp in summer—or ski, snowmobile or ice-fish in winter. These backroads can also provide alternate routes to other parts of the Okanagan "Wonderland".

•••

Fig. 2: The "Sails" by R. Dow Reid (Bernard and Abbott).

2

Knox Mountain

Statistics	For map, see page 20.
Distance:	6 km, Highway 97 to Knox Mtn Summit.
Travel Time:	10 to 15 minutes.
Elevation Gain:	306 metres.
Condition:	Paved throughout.
Season:	Year around. Could be slippery in winter.
Topo Maps:	Kelowna, B.C. 82 E/14 (1:50,000).
Communities:	Kelowna.

Hiking Trails in the Heart of Kelowna

Knox Mountain, named after Arthur Booth Knox, is a pleasant getaway only a few minutes north of downtown Kelowna. Viewpoints and trails near the 647 metre (2,123 foot) summit make the climb from the lakeshore, at 341 metres (1,119 feet) above sea level, well worthwhile, particularly as there is a paved road to the top.

In 1883 Arthur Knox, an immigrant from Aberdeenshire, Scotland, purchased a farm on the shores of Okanagan Lake, north of Mission Creek. He also acquired the mountain and land as far north as Okanagan Centre as rangeland. In 1904, Knox sold the bottomland to a syndicate developing the town of Kelowna.

Brass plaques on the mountain also honor Benjamin De Furlong Boyce, M.D. who gave 77 hectares (190 acres) to the city for the park and Stanley Merriam Simpson, a Kelowna industrialist, who funded much of its development.

Access to Knox Mountain Park is simple. If you are traveling through Kelowna on Highway 97 (Harvey Avenue), turn north on Ellis Street, three blocks east of the Okanagan Lake Floating Bridge. Follow

Ellis Street past the Kelowna Centennial Museum, the Orchard Museum and the beaches of Sutherland Park. (All worthwhile diversions if you are not in a hurry to get to the top.) The park gate and hill climb starts about 2.5 kilometres from Highway 97 (Harvey Avenue). A parking lot and viewpoint one kilometre up provides a place to rest and enjoy the view, particularly if your mode of transportation is self-propelled. A side road leads into picnic tables and a small playing field approximately 2.5 kilometres from the park gate and the main parking area. Viewpoints and shelters are another kilometre farther along, approximately six kilometres from Highway 97 (Harvey Avenue).

Trails skirt the mountain top and follow the hogs-back ridge to the north, providing an excellent view of Bear Creek Provincial Park and its canyon to the west and the long expanse of Okanagan Lake to the north. Wildflowers (and wood ticks) abound in April and May and the flowering rabbitbush can be particularly colorful in mid-September.

While the road and trails of Knox Mountain are usually the quiet domain of Sunday drivers, cyclists, joggers, hikers and plodders, the May holiday weekend is a distinct exception. The Knox Mountain Hill Climb, according to a story in the May 1, 1992, edition of the *Kelowna Capital News*, has been going on for 35 years.

"After successful events on hills in Penticton and Westbank, the OASC (Okanagan Auto Sports Club) applied for the use of the Knox Mountain Road in 1966. It quickly became obvious to drivers that this was a mean hill, only 18 feet wide and with steep cliffs on either side.

"The road rises 800 feet through 17 corners and adjoining straightaways. The course record was set by John Haftner in 1990 when he steered his TUI Super Vee up the incline in one minute, 46.893 seconds."

There are currently no maps available to detail the many footpaths on the mountain, but animal lovers should note that Knox Mountain Park is one of the few places where there are designated trails for walking dogs.

•••

Additional Information Sources

Kelowna Chamber of Commerce
544 Harvey Avenue,
Kelowna, B.C. V1Y 6C9
Tel: (604) 861-1515

•••

16

3

Woodhaven Nature Conservancy

Statistics	For maps, see pages 18 & 20.
Distance:	9 km south of downtown Kelowna.
Travel Time:	Approximately 15 minutes.
Condition:	Paved city streets.
Season:	Year around.
Topo Maps:	Kelowna, B.C. 82 E/14 (1:50,000).
Communities:	Kelowna and Okanagan Mission.

Kelowna's Best Kept Secret

Fig. 3: Nancy Wise and Joan Burbridge (L) at Woodhaven.

$\mathbb{T}$here's a hidden vale at the south end of Raymer Road in Kelowna's Okanagan Mission area that's an ideal place to take a quiet walk almost any time of the year. At just under nine hectares (21.6 acres), it certainly doesn't qualify as the largest park in the region and, unless you consider its permanent and transient natural residents, it certainly isn't likely to be the busiest. But, on an otherwise quiet spring morning, it can be one of the noisiest places around—if you consider the chatter of a squirrel and the raucous call of a jay noise.

The simplest way to find Woodhaven is to take Gordon Road south off Highway 97 (Harvey Avenue) near downtown Kelowna. Continue south past Mission Creek and then turn east on Raymer Road, 7.2 kilometres from Highway 97. Follow Raymer for another 1.8 kilometres as it zig-zags through Okanagan Mission to the Woodhaven gate. A large map on site amply details the trails and the various climatic zones they wind through. A walk around the perimeter of Woodhaven Nature Conservancy is less that 1.5 kilometres, but if you do it on a counter-clockwise direction, you will pass through a creek-bottom jungle, across a dry hillside (complete with prickly-pear cactus) and through an ancient cedar forest. If you're fortunate, you may find Joan Burbridge, Woodhaven's caretaker, on site and willing to answer a few of your questions.

•••

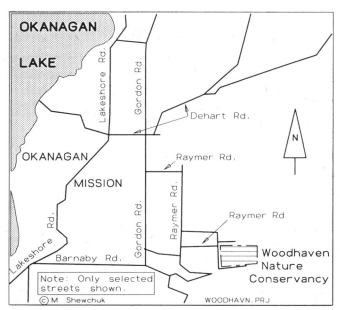

Information Sources.

Regional District of Central Okanagan 540 Groves Ave., Kelowna, B.C. V1Y 4Y7 Tel: 763-4918

•••

Map 1: Woodhaven Nature Conservancy area.

4

Bertram Creek Regional Park

Statistics	For map, see page 20.
Distance:	14 km from Hwy 97 (Harvey Avenue).
Travel Time:	About ½ hour. (See page 23 for access details.)
Condition:	Paved throughout.
Season:	Year around.
Topo Maps:	Kelowna, B.C. E/NW (1:100,000).
Communities:	Kelowna and Okanagan Mission.

Pack your Picnic Basket

Bertram Creek Regional Park, south of Kelowna on the east shore of Okanagan Lake, is deceptive. From the roadway, there is little to indicate the lush green lawns shaded by giant pine and fir. The sign doesn't tell you about the picnic tables scattered throughout the facility and the hedges of vine maple, wild rose, saskatoon and Oregon grape that act as natural sound barriers. It's easy to pass it by on your way to Okanagan Mountain Park without realizing that there is a 400-metre-long beach equipped with changehouses, toilets and a shelter or two to protect you from the sun or a sudden summer shower.

If you stop to listen, you might hear laughing children, chattering squirrels or a chickadee's distinctive song. If you pulled into the upper parking lot and looked closely, you might see groundsquirrels watching you intently from the mouths of their burrows. You might also see trails leading along a rocky headland or a roadway leading down toward Okanagan Lake. You might also see wildflowers in spring and ripe saskatoons at the end of June.

But then again, you might just drive by and miss it all.

•••

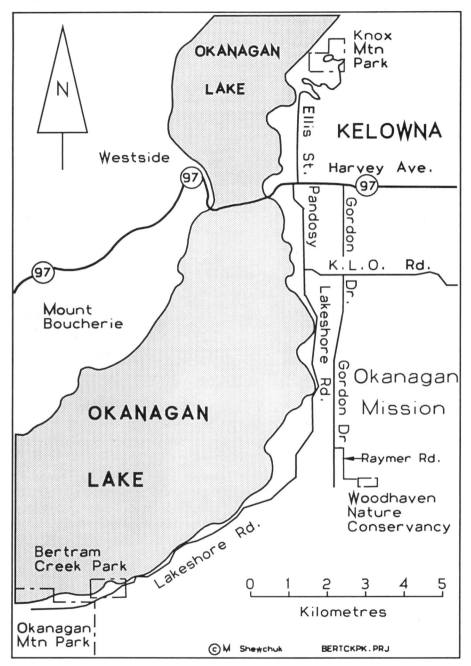

Map 2: Kelowna and Okanagan Mission area.

Okanagan Mountain Park

Statistics	For maps, see pages 20 & 22.
Distance:	20 km, Hwy 97, Kelowna to north entrance.
	27 km, Hwy 97, Penticton to south parking lot.
Travel Time:	Approx ½ hour from highway.
Condition:	Paved with some gravel sections.
Season:	South entrance may be closed in winter.
Topo Maps:	Peachland, B.C. 82 E/13 (1:50,000).
	Summerland, B.C. 82 E/12 (1:50,000).
Forest Maps:	Penticton and Area.
Communities:	Kelowna, Peachland and Penticton.

From Sagebrush to Huckleberries

Okanagan Mountain Provincial Park offers you a truly diverse spectrum of outdoor pursuits. Because of its large land mass and wide elevation range—1,200 metres (3,900 feet) between lakeshore and mountain summit—the park contains a wide variety of ecosystems. A semi-desert wilderness on the lakeshore headlands blends into lush, green forest in the sub-alpine plateau.

Secluded coves and sandy beaches highlight the park's Okanagan Lake shoreline, with six marine camping areas for overnight boat camping. Inland are spectacular Wildhorse Canyon and Goode's Creek Canyon, cutting deeply north and south through the mass of Okanagan Mountain. Over 24 kilometres of connecting trails suitable for hiking, mountain biking and horseback riding lead through the canyons and into four spring-fed mountain lakes located along forested upper mountain ridges. You may see mule deer, elk and black bear and even an occasional mountain goat and cougar. Ospreys build their massive aeries in the tall trees near Norman, Baker and Divide lakes.

21

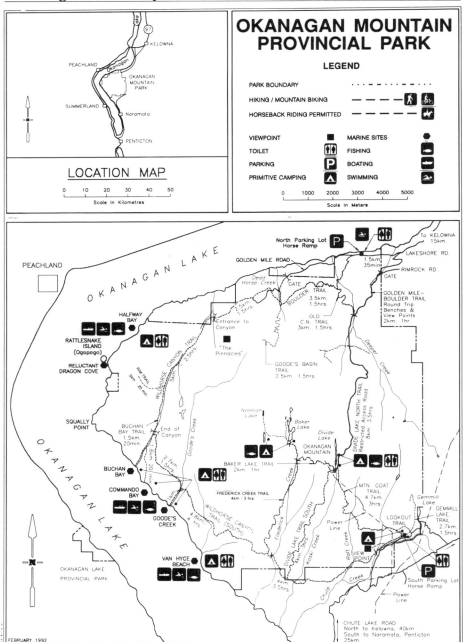

Map 3: Okanagan Mountain Park (Courtesy of B.C. Parks).

Established in 1973, after years of lobbying by the Okanagan Similkameen Parks Society, the park encompasses 10,462 hectares (25,841 acres) of wilderness on Okanagan Mountain and spectacularly rugged Okanagan Lake foreshore.

Okanagan Mountain Provincial Park has a fascinating cultural history as well. Indian pictographs can be found on canyon walls and outcrops in several places. Early missionaries, fur traders, cattlemen and miners traveled a series of now overgrown Okanagan Mountain trails more than a century and half ago. Scattered old homesteads are evidence of attempts to settle this rugged landscape. Horse-logging was common up until the 1930's, and cattle are still grazing on the eastern boundary of the park. Despite all the human activity, the park remains a relatively undisturbed wilderness area.

The northern boundary of Okanagan Mountain Park can be reached from Kelowna by turning south off Highway 97 (Harvey Avenue) on to Pandosy Street, a few blocks from the floating bridge (kilometre 0.0). Pandosy Street soon becomes Lakeshore Road as you follow it through Okanagan Mission, keeping right at the flashing light at the junction of Lakeshore and Chute Lake Road (km 9.0). If you are planning to spend a day or two in the hills, consider stopping for refreshments at the Cedar Creek Estate Winery near km 13.

Bertram Creek Regional Park, near km 14, is another recreational option on the way to the mountain. After a day of horse riding, hiking or mountain biking, it may be a necessary stop for a swim before facing the city. (See Bertram Creek Park on page 19 for more information.)

Rimrock Road, near km 15, provides access to the start of the Divide Lake Trailhead. This 10 kilometre route follows an old microwave site access road to Divide Lake and the peak of Okanagan Mountain. A gate two kilometres up Rimrock Road bars vehicles from using the microwave site access road and parking is limited to only a few vehicles.

About two kilometres farther along Lakeshore Road is a parking lot and entrance sign to Okanagan Mountain Park. There are toilets, a horse loading ramp and a swimming beach nearby, but no overnight camping.

After passing through several small subdivisions, Lakeshore Road ends at km 20 in a wide cul-de-sac. Parking here is also limited, but a very rough, enticing trail angles down to the lake. A few hundred metres before the end of the road, a sign on the hillside marks the start of the ancient trail into the upper end of Wildhorse Canyon. The trail, though wide and easily navigated on foot or mountain bicycle, climbs steadily, gaining about 200 metres in two kilometres before leveling off. Near the crest it is joined by portions of the Boulder Trail and Goode's Basin

23

Trail. An up-to-date map, available from B.C. Parks, and topographic maps are essential before heading too far into the north end of the park.

Fig. 4: Prickly-pear cactus in blossom.

O kanagan Mountain Park has approximately 25 kilometres (15.5 miles) of unobstructed shoreline with ready access to the trail system at Buchan Bay, Commando Bay and Goode's Creek. The south-facing slopes surrounding these access points are classic examples of the dry environment that is said by some to be a northern extension of the Sonoran Desert of the southern U.S.A. Sagebrush, bunchgrass, prickly-pear cactus, ponderosa pine and poison ivy eke out an existence where-ever moisture gathers. Pacific rattlesnakes are frequently sighted along the trail, but given a wide berth, they tend to be wary of humans.

The Commando Bay trail, across the slopes and into the foot of Wildhorse Canyon, is an easy, picturesque walk that is best tackled in early morning before the sun turns the sheltered draws into a bake-oven. The canyon trail is a pleasant walk along an old road that was once promoted as the ideal route for a highway from Kelowna to Penticton. Wilderness lovers should be thankful that saner heads prevailed.

Several trails offer access to the southern part of the park from Penticton and Naramata via Naramata Road and Chute Lake Road. With the five-way junction of Main Street, Westminster Avenue and Front Street in downtown Penticton as km "0", follow Front Street northeast to Vancouver Avenue, then follow the signs to Naramata. Continue past Naramata to Chute Lake Road (km 20), then follow the steeply climbing Chute Lake Road for another five kilometres to the Gemmill Lake Road (marked with a sign to Okanagan Mountain Park). A narrow road winds through the evergreens for another 1.6 km to the South Parking Lot and a tenting campground near Chute Creek.

Fig. 5: Divide Lake in Okanagan Mountain Park.

The Mountain Goat Trail, in the southeast sector of Okanagan Mountain Park, is aptly named. It starts off at the south parking lot, accessible from Chute Lake Road, and climbs steadily through semi-open timber to Divide Lake, just east of Okanagan Mountain summit. In keeping with the park's role to conserve the wilderness experience, the trail has no graveled pathways and no toilets along the way. It is unsuitable for mountain bicycles and a challenge to skilled horsemen on skilled horses. It is a steady climb up and around granite bluffs, over boulders and between trees.

The B.C. Parks map says the trail is 4.7 km long and a three hour hike—one way. Add another half an hour if you're over 40. You can also count on one half to three quarters of that time for the return trip.

Although Divide Lake is a cool, clear spring-fed lake at an elevation of 1,500 metres (4,900 feet), carry plenty of water. For a mid-summer jaunt up the Mountain Goat Trail, plan on carrying at least one litre of water per hiker. There are no trustworthy creeks along the way—in fact, most of the creek beds are likely to be bone dry. Because of the wildlife in the park, the water is also likely to be unsafe even if it is flowing.

If you haven't been frightened off by this preamble, you are probably tough enough to enjoy this hike. Among the reasons to consider it is the relatively short distance from your vehicle to the heart of the park plus the opportunity for a cool, private swim in an upland tarn. An additional reason to make the climb is the relatively easy access to Baker and Norman lakes. Both lakes have excellent fishing for pan-sized trout and are downhill from Divide Lake.

From a naturalist's or photographer's perspective, getting there *is* half the fun. The trail starts off in a damp upland environment with evergreens, alder and vine maple shading queen's cup, thimbleberry and star-flowered Solomon's seal. Oregon grape grow profusely at all elevations along the trail. As you climb away from Chute Creek, the growth reflects the drier climate. White bunchberry blossoms, columbine and lupines add color to the slopes in early summer, later replaced by the red bunchberries and black huckleberries that could add a dainty touch to your bannock.

Not everyone thinks of food when they hike—poor souls. If scenic views turn you on, you'll be able to catch a few glimpses Giants Head Mountain and the south end of Okanagan Lake. But Divide Lake is the real beauty up here. It is a steep-sided mountain crevice filled with cool, clear green water. It will take you about fifteen minutes to walk the length of it, skirting the six-metre cliffs that make up the east shore. You may find a few ledges suitable for sunbathing or fishing, but you won't find a beach. There are, however, a few picnic tables, a pit toilet and a fine little cabin with no doors.

●●●

Additional Information Sources:

B.C. Parks
P.O. Box 399,
Summerland, B.C. V0H 1Z0

Okanagan Similkameen Parks
Society, P.O. Box 787,
Summerland, B.C. V0H 1Z0

●●●

6
─

Chute Lake Loop

Statistics   **For maps, see pages 43 & 29.**

Distance:	77 km, Hwy 97, Kelowna to Hwy 97, Penticton.
Travel Time:	Two to four hours.
Condition:	Some rough gravel, may be closed in winter.
Season:	July through October.
Topo Maps:	Kelowna, B.C. 82 E/NW (1:100,000).
	Kelowna, B.C. 82 E/14 (1:50,000).
	Summerland, B.C. 82 E/12 (1:50,000).
Forest Maps:	Penticton and Area.
Communities:	Kelowna, Naramata and Penticton.

Follow the Kettle Valley Line

The Kettle Valley Railway right-of-way, between McCulloch Station and Naramata, has become a favorite travel route for motorcyclists, mountain bicyclists and backroad explorers. Because of the easy grades and spectacular scenery, efforts have been under way for several years to have the route preserved and maintained as a linear park.

It should be emphasized that this is presently a "travel at your own risk" route. At the time of writing, parts of the railway right-of-way were being used as an active logging road, other parts were not being maintained in any significant way, and still other sections (particularly the tunnels and trestles) were of questionable safety. Fortunately, the trestles can be avoided by gaining access to the KVR right-of-way via the Gillard Creek F.S. Road and a trail and short side road bypass the slowly-deteriorating Adra Tunnel. The hazards, however, have done little to discourage cyclists from making the long, scenic run from McCulloch Road or Gillard Creek Road to Naramata.

27

Fig. 6: Cyclists on the Bellevue Creek Trestle.

From a lazy man's perspective, the most enjoyable direction to follow the KVR route is from high above Kelowna, down to Naramata, particularly if you are on a bicycle. With the junction of Highway 97 (Harvey Avenue) and Pandosy Street as your kilometre 0.0 reference, follow Pandosy Street south, continuing on this main route as it becomes Lakeshore Road. Leave Lakeshore Road where it makes a right turn at the flashing light at km 9. Follow Chute Lake Road up the hill to Hedeman Road, at km 11, being careful not to turn on Oakview Road. Turn left on Hedeman Road and look for the entrance to the Gillard Creek F.S. Road, opposite the Cedar Creek #6 Firehall.

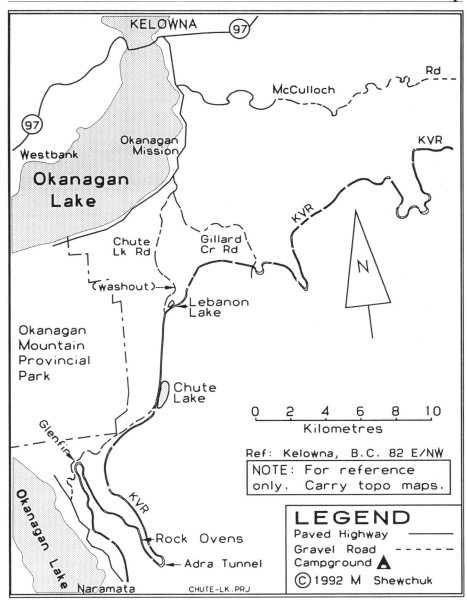

Map 4: Chute Lake Road and the Kettle Valley Railway.

The Gillard Creek Road, despite its inauspicious beginnings, is a well-used forest access road. Although steep and dusty, with a few switchback turns and narrow sections thrown in for excitement, it should pose few difficulties in dry weather. As a safety precaution, it may be smart to leave the road to the logging trucks on weekdays.

At one time, the regular route from Kelowna to Chute Lake was via the Chute Lake Road, but by the summer of 1991, it was virtually blocked by a major washout 8.5 kilometres from the junction with Lakeshore Road. A bypass had been chewed around the washout, but it was too steep for two-wheel drive vehicles and many normal 4x4's.

After climbing approximately 700 metres (2,300 feet) in the 8.5 kilometres from the fire hall to the KVR right-of-way, the time comes to make a decision. If you're planning a bicycle trip to Naramata, you can follow the right-of-way east (up the track) for a few hundred metres to a wide, safe parking area near the old Gillard Creek trestle, and begin your cycle touring. If you decide to continue left (east), the tall, curved steel Bellevue Creek trestle is about 4.5 kilometres east of the Gillard Creek Road/KVR junction and is well worth a visit. Cyclists and light vehicles were crossing it in the summer of 1991. However, because the trestle ties are spaced about 20 centimetres (eight inches) apart and there are no length-wise planks, it is certainly no place for a Sunday walk, particularly if you are afraid of heights. A network of logging roads and trails leads from the east side of the trestle southeast past Crawford Lake to the 2,137 metre (7,011 foot) summit of Little White Mountain. It's about 9.5 kilometres from the trestle to the summit. Information on this and other hiking trails in the area is available from the Regional District of the Central Okanagan in Kelowna.

If you choose to go right (west) at the Gillard Creek Road/KVR junction you can begin the gradual descent to Chute Lake and Naramata. The right-of-way is fairly narrow with little room to pass a cyclist, let alone a logging truck or another vehicle. Fortunately, visibility is generally good and there are frequent wide sections to pull over.

Lebanon Lake, approximately 26 kilometres from downtown Kelowna (Hwy 97), is the first major landmark on the now-southward descent. The rough road to the west at the south end of the lake is the continuation of the old Chute Lake Road. If you are riding a mountain bicycle or a 4x4 with excellent clearance, you could consider returning to the Cedar Creek #6 Firehall via this route, but there are no guarantees the road will be easy, or even passable.

The KVR right-of-way continues south another 5.5 kilometres to the Chute Lake Resort at the former site of the Chute Lake station. At an elevation of 1,160 metres (3,950 feet) Chute Lake can be a cool oasis in a hot Okanagan summer—or a snowmobiling haven in a dry Okanagan winter.

30

Gary and Doreen Reed have operated the Chute Lake Resort since 1975, catering to fishermen, hunters, snowmobilers, cross-country skiers and just plain vacationers who want to get away from the city for a weekend. Chute Lake, says Gary Reed, is high enough and cool enough to keep the rainbow trout firm and tasty year around. To make it easier for the drop-in fisherman, the resort offers log cabins, lodge accommodation, campsites and a licensed dining room, if you aren't into cooking. Gasoline- and electric-powered motorboats, canoes and rowboats as well as fishing tackle are also available.

Bring up the subject of hunting, and Gary Reed will show you the snapshots of the #3 and #5 record Boone & Crockett whitetail bucks taken in the nearby mountains. According to Gary, George West of Victoria took the #3 buck (a B&C score of 173) in 1987. Fred Metter, also of Victoria, took the #5 buck that same year with a B&C score of 169 $7/_8$ points. He will also tell you about the herd of elk that is attracting plenty of attention. Moose, once a scarcity this far south, are now thriving in the upland marshes.

The junction at the south end of Chute Lake is a place for decision making. You can follow the steep, winding gravel road for about 11 kilometres down to Naramata Road and a further 20 kilometres south to downtown Penticton. Or you can follow the steady grade of the Kettle Valley Railway as it snakes down the mountain, passing two tunnels, rock ovens and spectacular viewpoints before reaching a man-made dead-end at Smethurst Road above Naramata. If your mode of transport is a bicycle, motorcycle or smaller vehicle (motorhomes are out), AND if there are no new washouts or cave-ins, the KVR right-of-way is the only interesting choice.

With the junction at the gate of Chute Lake Resort as your kilometre 0.0 reference (add about 32 kilometres to the following references if you're fixed on Highway 97 in Kelowna as km 0.0), follow the railway grade as it carves a gentle arc across the mountainside. You'll have the option of rejoining Chute Lake Road near km 2.5 and again via the Elinor Lake F.S. Road near km 9.3. Watch for the foundation of a railway water tank near km 10.5 and the extra wide right-of-way of the passing track of Adra before reaching the 489 metre (1,604 foot) long Adra Tunnel. The tunnel carves a curve within the mountain and a weak spot in the roof near the mid-point is slowly caving in. At last check, the tunnel had been barricaded and a hiking/biking trail bypasses it. The Elinor Lake Road, mentioned earlier, can also be used to get down to the next level of the right-of-way.

31

The right-of-way now traverses the mountainside in a northwesterly direction. Watch for a wide spot in the grade near km 14.8 just before it enters a rock cut. If you've found the right wide spot, you can park and follow a fairly well-used trail up the hillside to a fine specimen of the rock ovens that once served the railway construction crews. (If you bypassed the tunnel via Elinor Lake Road, back-track a few hundred metres up the railway grade.) According to several sources, including Bob Gibbard of nearby Glenfir, these ovens were used by the railway construction camp cooks during 1912 and 1913 when baking for the hungry, hardworking crews. A regional park has been established to protect these unique ovens as relics of an important part of our past. Although we only managed to find one complete oven on our trip down the KVR, Bob Gibbard suggests that there are half a dozen such locations between Chute Lake and Naramata.

Elinor Lake F.S. Road again crosses the right-of-way at km 15 and between that crossing and the hairpin turn at Glenfir (km 20.8) there are several opportunities to photograph Naramata and Okanagan Lake with the next traverse of the railway far below. A short, dusty side road at Glenfir also provides the opportunity to rejoin Chute Lake Road.

There are several more excellent viewpoints near km 24, but one of the most spectacular is at the mouth of the Little Tunnel at km 25.5. Below you to the south, the scattered ponderosa pine and bunchgrass gives way to the neatly manicured orchards of Naramata and then the beaches and cityscape of Penticton. Skaha Lake disappears around the bend on the horizon. The winding descent on the KVR right-of-way ends at Smethurst Road at km 30 (Naramata Creek F.S. Road on the uphill side) and after leaving the KVR, it's little more than a kilometre down Smethurst Road to Naramata Road.

If you've made the trip on a hot, dusty day, it's less than a kilometre to Robinson Avenue and then two kilometres downhill to Naramata's fine beaches. Highway 97 and the beaches at the foot of Okanagan Lake in Penticton are about 14 kilometres south of the junction of Smethurst Road and Naramata Road.

• • •

Additional Information Sources:

Chute Lake Resort
RR #1, Box 16, Site 16,
Naramata, B.C. V0H 1N0
Tel. (604) 493-3535

• • •

West Kettle Route—Highway 33

Statistics	For map, see page 34.
Distance:	129 km, Hwy 33, Rutland to Rock Creek.
Travel Time:	Approximately two hours.
Elevation Gain:	Approximately 925 metres.
Condition:	Paved throughout, some steep grades.
Season:	Open year around.
Topo Maps:	Kelowna 82 E/NW (1:100,000).
	Penticton 82 E/SE (1:100,000).
	Grand Forks 82 E/SE (1:100,000).
Communities:	Kelowna, Osoyoos & Rock Creek.

Silver, Snow and the KVR

Placer gold, fingers of silver, an abandoned railway and a ski resort that rivals Europe's best may appear to be an unusual combination, but a little known B.C. highway provides access to all of them and much more.

British Columbia's 129-kilometre-long Highway 33 links the central Okanagan with the Boundary Region. On the way, it passes through the West Kettle River valley—a dry, timbered region varied and colorful in both scenery and history. This is a quiet part of the province; a part that has a charm and grace still unspoiled by the hustle and bustle of the 1990s. Ranchers, loggers, retired hard-rock miners and railroaders still enjoy the company of their friends and neighbors—and any strangers that take the time to chat.

The north end of Highway 33 begins at the junction with Highway 97 in Rutland, a Kelowna suburb. Highway 33 ends at Rock Creek, at the junction with Crowsnest Highway 3 near the Canada-U.S.A. boundary, 52 kilometres east of Osoyoos.

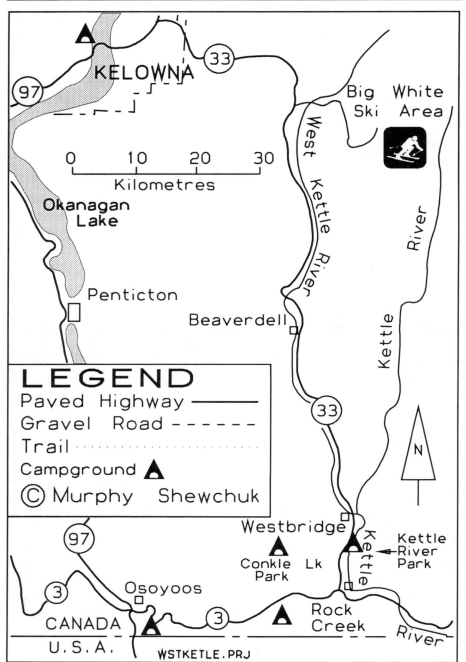

Map 5: West Kettle Road (Highway 33).

Text within map:

KELOWNA

97

33

Big White
Ski Area

West Kettle River

River

Kettle

0 10 20 30
Kilometres

Okanagan
Lake

Penticton

Beaverdell

33

N

LEGEND
Paved Highway ——————
Gravel Road - - - - - -
Trail ·····················
Campground ▲
© Murphy Shewchuk

97

Westbridge

Conkle Lk
Park

Kettle

Kettle River Park

3

Osoyoos

CANADA
U.S.A.

3

Rock
Creek

River

WSTKETLE.PRJ

[Just a word of warning, the next gasoline service station is at Beaverdell, 79 kilometres down the road.]

Highway 33 passes through the heart of downtown Rutland before beginning a steady southeast climb out of the Okanagan Valley. The land of orchards and blue water is quickly left behind. Golden rangeland and chokecherry and saskatoon bushes replace the peach and apple orchards that have helped make the Okanagan Valley famous.

After allowing one last glimpse of the sprawling city below, the road opens to a view of the timber-lined canyon of Mission Creek. Originally named Riviere L'Anse du Sable by the fur traders, Mission Creek was a busy gold placer creek for a short time in the mid-1870s. According to historian and now B.C. M.L.A. N.L. "Bill" Barlee, Dan Gallagher, the last of the old prospectors, eked out a living on the creek until the 1940s.

Approximately 24 kilometres east of Kelowna, the highway crosses Mission Creek and enters the Joe Rich Valley. During the period between the two World Wars the remarkably rich black soil of the valley supported a lettuce market gardening industry. E.O. MacGinnis started the lettuce farming and made a fortune before everybody got into it, says one old-timer. The Joe Rich Community Centre marks the heart of the former market gardening enclave. There are only a few families living here now who work and live off their land as ranchers. Most of the people here work in Kelowna, but prefer living in the country.

Less than 10 minutes beyond the Joe Rich Valley community center, a junction marks the paved road that leads 24 kilometres east and up to Big White Ski Resort. From a ski resort started in the early 1960s, Big White has become the closest a westerner can get to a European ski experience. It is a ski village in the mountains, equipped with private chalets, condominium style apartments, and a hotel complex with ski-to-your-door accommodations for over 2,000 guests. A choice of restaurants, discos, lounges and a grocery store help round out the facilities. Oh yes! Chair lifts and T-bar lifts, numerous downhill runs plus cross country ski trails on top of 12 metres of average snowfall help complete the requirements for a memorable ski holiday.

Just beyond the Big White junction is the Rock Creek—Kelowna Summit. At an elevation of 1,265 meters (4,159 feet) it marks

35

the divide between the Okanagan and West Kettle drainage basins. The summit also marks a change in the scenery from the narrow valley of Mission and Joe Rich creeks to a broader, drier valley, lightly timbered with aspen and pine.

Five kilometers past the summit, there is another major junction, this time to the right. A well-maintained logging road continues south past Idabel Lake, and a secondary road parallels a weed-overgrown railroad bed as far as McCulloch Station before the railbed strikes across the mountainside to Penticton and the road winds down the mountainside to Kelowna. (See *McCulloch Road*, page 41 for details.)

U nder the direction of Chief Engineer Andrew McCulloch, construction of the Kettle Valley Railway (KVR), a Canadian Pacific Railway subsidiary, was begun in the summer of 1910. By the end of 1913, tracks had been laid from Midway in the Boundary region to Mile 83, a short distance west of McCulloch Station. This long-awaited Coast-to-Kootenay railway was finally completed through the Coquihalla Canyon (north of Hope) on July 31, 1916.

Steam buffs will undoubtedly remember the Kettle Valley Railway as one of the last bastions of "real" railroading. With speeds that varied from 25 kilometres per hour (15 mph) on the tortuous mountain grades to 90 kilometres per hour (55 mph) on the flat valley floors, steam led the way. The Mikados, the Consolidations and a few old Ten-Wheelers pulled passengers and freight over some of the most difficult terrain in North America. In its heyday, the steam-driven cylinders powered the eastbound Kettle Valley Express from Vancouver through Hope, Penticton, Rock Creek, Midway and on to Nelson in 23 hours. In another five hours, the "Express" had arrived at Medicine Hat, Alberta.

A large washout permanently closed the Coquihalla section of the KVR in 1959 and the last passenger run from Penticton to Midway took place in 1964. Since then, despite protests and suggestions that the route could be operated as a tourist attraction, the tracks have been removed on the Penticton-Midway section, as well as the Coquihalla and much of the route between Okanagan Falls and Spences Bridge.

B ack on Highway 33, about 73 kilometres south of Kelowna, the paved road passes the recently-collapsed weathered shell of the former Carmi School. There is little else to indicate that, in 1914, Carmi had two hotels, two stores, a shoe shop, a resident policeman and jail, and a railroad hospital. The railway and a gold mine were the source of income in Carmi. When the mine closed in 1936, the town was dealt a severe blow. The closure of the railway finished it off.

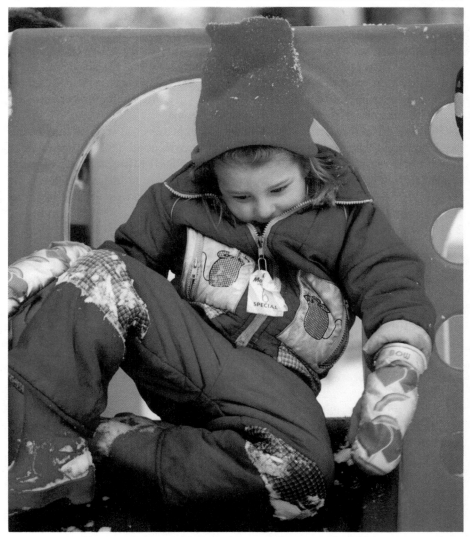

Fig. 7: Taking a break from skiing at Big White.

Six kilometres south of Carmi, on the outskirts of Beaverdell, the East Beaver Creek Road begins a winding route eastward around Curry Mountain to Christian Valley. If you're interested in a little backcountry exploring, there is a network of logging roads and a dozen Forest Service recreation sites in the mountains between Beaverdell and Christian Valley. The Boundary District Forest Service Recreation Sites map, available from most Forest Service offices in the area, has the details.

37

There have been silver mines on Wallace Mountain, to the east of Beaverdell, since before the turn of the century. The first claim was staked on the mountain in 1889, but was apparently allowed to lapse. In 1896, a flurry of staking took place and the West Kettle River soon saw three new communities, including Carmi, Beaverton and Rendell. Later Beaverton and Rendell, only a short distance apart, were united under the name of Beaverdell.

Several mines operated profitably during the first half of the twentieth century. The Bell Mine, for instance, produced 350,000 ounces of silver between 1913 and 1936. The Highland Bell Mine, the site of more recent activities, was formed in 1936 through the amalgamation of the Bell and the Highland Lass claims. The silver was in veins "like the fingers on his hand," remembered miner Charlie Pasco of the day in 1945, when he first came to work for the old Highland Bell.

The pub in the Beaverdell Hotel, itself a museum piece, is certainly one of the more colourful places to visit in the community, particularly on a Friday or Saturday night. Several of the walls are decorated with large-size black and white photographs of pioneer hotels in the Boundary district.

Logging is the main industry of the West Kettle Valley today. The majority of timber harvested is jackpine and, according to one logger, most of it is hauled by truck to the mill at Midway.

Throughout the length of Highway 33 there are many spots where self-contained recreational vehicles can park for the night. However, the first privately-operated roadside campground on the southward journey is the West Kettle Campground, 16 kilometres south of Beaverdell. It is a inviting location, laid out among the pines.

A kilometre or two farther south, a gravel road winds westward to Conkle Lake Provincial Park. See *Conkle Lake Loop*, page 119.

The West Kettle River and the Kettle River join at Westbridge. A secondary road follows the Kettle River northward, past the settlement of Christian Valley, eventually joining Highway 6 near Monashee Pass, east of Lumby.

A short drive south of Westbridge lies the Kettle River Provincial Park campground. Set in the pines at a bend on the west bank of the river, this picturesque spot contains 49 campsites, picnic tables and an opportunity to swim, fish or cycle. The area is also ideal for the artist or photographer. In the summer months, the nearby irrigated hay fields are lush green, while outside the range of the sprinklers, the foliage is typical of the interior semi-desert plateau country.

Rock Creek is the southern terminus of Highway 33 and the end of the 129 kilometre drive from Kelowna—plus side trips, of course. Rock Creek was also the best-known placer gold creek in the Boundary region of British Columbia. Discovered in 1859 by Adam Beam, the creek was worked extensively from 1860 to 1864. At the peak of activity at least 500 miners scoured its gravels. Historians estimate that well over 250,000 ounces of gold—then worth $16 per ounce—was recovered from the creek before the paydirt played out and the miners moved north to the Cariboo. The creek saw limited action again during the recessions of the 1890s and 1930s. With the present price of gold, and the state of the B.C. economy, there may again be prospectors searching for the elusive Mother Lode.

Today, Rock Creek is the center of a busy agricultural community. Patient ewes and prancing lambs liven up the fields in the spring, while the yellow arrowleaf balsamroot brighten the open slopes.

Midway, 19 kilometres east of Rock Creek on Crowsnest Highway 3, is well worth the visit regardless of your ultimate direction. The Kettle River Museum, officially opened in Midway in 1977, is an excellent source of information on the history of the Kettle Valley.

The West Kettle Route—Highway 33—seems left out of the hustle and bustle of today. But, if you are interested in a skiing holiday, or a camping, fishing or back-country exploring vacation, this may be an advantage—not a disadvantage.

•••

Additional Information Sources:

Kelowna Chamber of Commerce
544 Harvey Avenue,
Kelowna, B.C. V1Y 6C9
Tel. (604) 861-1515

B.C. Parks
West Kootenay District,
RR 3, 4750 Highway 3A,
Nelson, B.C. V1L 5P6

•••

Fig. 8: Carmi School in September, 1984.

8

McCulloch Road

<table>
<tr><td colspan="2">Statistics   For map, see page 43.</td></tr>
<tr><td>Distance:</td><td>40 km, Highway 33 to downtown Kelowna.</td></tr>
<tr><td>Travel Time:</td><td>Up to one hour.</td></tr>
<tr><td>Elev. descent:</td><td>Approximately 925 metres.</td></tr>
<tr><td>Condition:</td><td>Gravel road with some steep sections.</td></tr>
<tr><td>Season:</td><td>May be closed in winter, slippery when wet.</td></tr>
<tr><td>Topo Maps:</td><td>Kelowna, B.C. 82 E/NW (1:100,000).</td></tr>
<tr><td>Forest Maps:</td><td>Penticton and Area.</td></tr>
<tr><td>Communities:</td><td>Kelowna, Rutland and Okanagan Mission.</td></tr>
</table>

Backroad with a View

If you're looking for some fishing, backroad exploring and beautiful scenic views—with the option to explore a few KVR trestles or strap on the cross-country skis, McCulloch Road is the answer. The upper or east end of McCulloch Road begins at Highway 33 in the West Kettle Valley, 40 kilometres southeast of the junction of Highway 97 and Highway 33 in Rutland, or six kilometres south of the junction to the Big White Ski Resort. (See *West Kettle Route*, page 33, for details.)

With the junction of Highway 33 and McCulloch Road as kilometre 0.0, the first major side road is less than one kilometre to the northwest. The well-maintained forest road to the south will take you past Haynes Lake and Idabel Lake Resort. If you follow it far enough, you can descend to the Okanagan Valley at Okanagan Falls with opportunities to fish, hike and explore along the way. However, as this is an active logging road it would be wise to restrict your exploring to weekends.

Staying on McCulloch Road, a junction at km 4.5 marks a short side road leading south to the Hydraulic (McCulloch) Lake reservoir and several small Forest Service recreation sites. Fishing in summer and

41

cross-country skiing in winter are the two main pursuits of the area. The lakes have been altered to serve as reservoirs for the massive amounts of water needed by the orchards in the Okanagan Valley near Kelowna.

The trackless remains of the Kettle Valley Railway (KVR) parallel the road for a short distance before continuing the descent to Naramata and Penticton, via Chute Lake. McCulloch Station, near km 6.0, served as the KVR station for Kelowna. Stage coaches and freight wagons made the hair-raising trip to and from the orchard community on a regular basis. See the *West Kettle Road* section, page 33, for more information on Andrew McCulloch and the Kettle Valley Railway.

A rough side road near km 8.5 leads south to the KVR right-of-way. Sight-seers and cyclists are often seen exploring the old KVR trestles along the section overlooking Kelowna. The view is spectacular, but the trestles can be extremely dangerous, so use caution.

A forest insect kill has made the area near km 17 a favored haunt of firewood cutters. The forest is also home to at least one family of black bears who enjoy the lush roadside growth. Remnants of wooden irrigation flumes can also be seen as the road descends into the Okanagan Valley. A rough side road through the trees near km 21 leads to an opening and an excellent view of East Kelowna with basalt columns in the foreground and Mount Boucherie and Westbank in the distance.

Beyond the viewpoint, the road descends through a mix of grasslands and light timber on the fringe of the valley. Switchback turns provide a bit of excitement for those unfamiliar with mountain roads, but good brakes and extra caution is all that is really needed to make the descent.

The basalt columns that were far below at the viewpoint a few minutes earlier are now just across a narrow valley near km 24. A short distance farther along, the road crosses Hydraulic Creek as it carries whatever water hasn't been used for irrigation purposes.

In 1890, in what was probably the first move towards irrigating the dry benches above Kelowna, the Lequimes built an irrigation ditch from what was then called Canyon Creek, near km 28, to the upper bench that is now East Kelowna. The Kelowna Land and Orchard Company (K.L.O.), formed in 1904, bought up the Lequime estate and with it the irrigation system. The water system is now part of the South East Kelowna Irrigation District.

The gravel of McCulloch Road gives way to pavement just before Gallagher's Canyon golf course (km 29). The grasslands are now invaded by a beautiful golf course and, farther down the road, by vineyards that soak in the sun on the slopes.

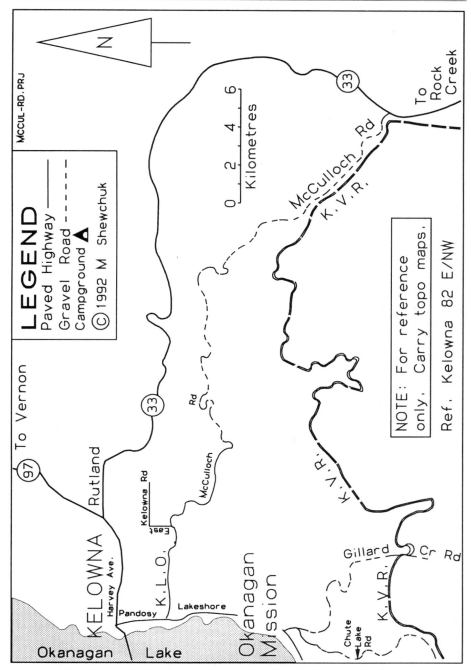

Map 6: McCulloch Road and the Kettle Valley Railway.

A viewpoint of the city of Kelowna (km 33) with its orchards and a backdrop of hills to the west presents still another reason why this is the largest community in the Okanagan Valley. McCulloch Road ends a short distance farther along, but if you wish to continue down toward Kelowna and Highway 97, follow K.L.O. Road west after crossing Mission Creek.

First known as Riviere L'Anse du Sable, Mission Creek took its present name from the settlement first established in 1860 by Father Pandosy. The Priests' ranch at Okanagan Mission is believed to be one of the first in the area to use irrigation with water rights on Mission Creek issued in April, 1874.

Mission Creek Regional Park, in the centre of greater Kelowna, is well worth a side trip. The 92 hectare (230 acre) park contains over 12 kilometres of hiking trails, a childrens' playground and a kokanee spawning channel—all in a mixed forest and river setting. To get there, turn north on Benvoulin Road and then east on Springfield Road.

Turn left (south) on Benvoulin Road, km 37, to explore the Pandosy Mission grounds near the corner of Benvoulin Road and Casorso Road. Casorso Road winds northwest to join K.L.O. Road, which in turn runs into Pandosy. After exploring the Pandosy Mission, you can also turn north on Benvoulin Road to Highway 97, a distance of about four kilometres. If you continue on K.L.O. Road at the Benvoulin Road junction, turn right on Pandosy and it will take you Harvey Avenue (Highway 97). If you are now totally confused, stop at the Kelowna Chamber of Commerce office for a city map before heading for the hills.

• • •

Additional Information Sources

Regional District of Central Okanagan
540 Groves Avenue,
Kelowna, B.C. V1Y 4Y7
Tel: (604) 763-4918

Kelowna Chamber of Commerce
544 Harvey Avenue,
Kelowna, B.C. V1Y 6C9
Tel. (604) 861-1515

• • •

9

Bear Creek Park

Statistics	For map, see page 64 & 46.
Distance:	7 km: Highway 97 to Bear Creek Park.
Travel Time:	Approximately 10 minutes.
Condition:	Paved with some narrow sections.
Season:	Year around.
Topo Maps:	Kelowna, B.C. 82 E/NW (1:100,000).
Forest Maps:	Penticton and area.
Communities:	Kelowna and Westbank.

Wild Canyons to Waterfront

Bear Creek Provincial Park is situated on the west side of Okanagan Lake, opposite the city of Kelowna. To reach it, turn west off Highway 97, two kilometres south of the floating bridge, and follow Westside Road north for seven kilometres. The park can also be reached from Vernon, by driving west on Highway 97 in the direction of Kamloops, and then turning south on Westside Road near O'Keefe Historic Ranch. Bear Creek Park is 57 kilometres south of the junction.

Founded in 1981, it takes in 167 hectares (413 acres) of some of the most interesting parkland in the Okanagan Valley. Once an integral part of Bear Creek Ranch, the Okanagan Lake shoreline provides several sheltered bays which are used for storing floating logs. The S.M. Simpson Sawmill Company purchased the site from the ranch for its logs, and later sold it to Crown Zellerbach Canada Limited which continued to use it for the same purpose. In 1981, British Columbia purchased the land from Crown Zellerbach for a provincial park. As a condition of sale, Crown Zellerbach maintained the rights to continue its booming activities north and south of the main beaches.

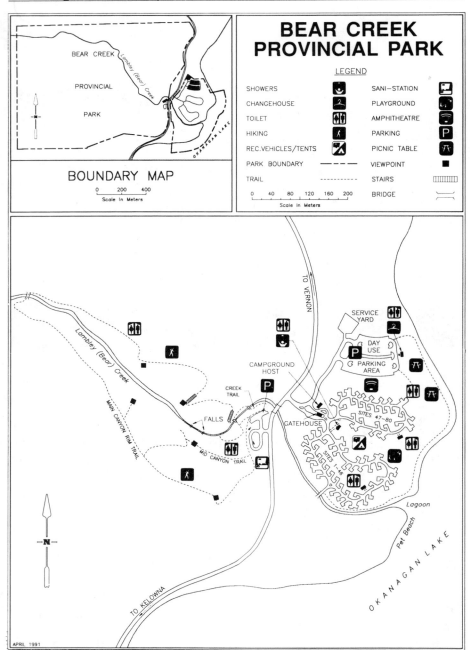

Map 7: Bear Creek Park (Courtesy of B.C. Parks).

Bear Creek Park is a natural wonderland. To the east of Westside Road are its beautiful sandy beaches and the level parkland which makes up the main campground. To the west, a spectacular canyon cuts through the rugged, rocky hills. The clear, cold waters of Bear Creek flow through the bottom of this steep-walled canyon, bringing with them small flakes of placer gold.

Above the canyon, ponderosa pine and Douglas fir dominate the dry, rocky hills and communities of juniper, bunchgrass, Indian paintbrush, arrowleaf balsamroot, Oregon grape and prickly-pear cactus compete for the area's meagre rainfall.

Below, in the shady confines of the canyon, moistened by the mist rising off the waterfalls, is yet another world. It is one of maple and birch, of saskatoon and chokecherry, of wild rose, horsetail and moss.

Wildlife abounds here. Violet-green swallows swoop gracefully through the canyon, red-tailed hawks ride warm afternoon updrafts high above, and owls hoot the night away as they have for centuries. The tree-frogs are noisiest in the spring, the crickets in the summer and the voices of the coyotes occasionally drift down from the hills to break the evening quiet.

The park contains over 400 metres of sandy beaches and 23 kilometres of well-marked hiking trails. Note that there are some very steep cliffs along the canyon walls. For safety reasons, you would be wise to stay on the trails when hiking. A loop hike from the trail parking lot, up the south side of the canyon on the mid-canyon trail to the canyon rim and then upstream to the footbridge presents an excellent example of typical north-slope environment in desert country. The walk back down the north side of the canyon is much drier. If you look closely, you may notice the remnants of an old irrigation ditch near viewpoint #5. Viewpoint #6 provides an excellent perspective for photographing the string of waterfalls on the canyon floor. Because of the west-east flow of the canyon, early to mid-morning could be the best time of the day to get your prize-winning photographs.

There are 80 campsites at present, a large picnic area, fire pits, showers and washrooms with flush toilets. Interpretive programs are provided from mid-June to early September at the amphitheatre.

You can fish Okanagan Lake for rainbow trout, whitefish, or kokanee. If fishing doesn't interest you, try hiking, swimming or boating. If you are very lucky, you may even catch a glimpse of the legendary Ogopogo, the lake monster said to live in the area.

●●●

Fig. 9: Hikers on a bridge across Lambly (Bear) Creek.

Additional Information Available From:

B.C. Parks
P.O. Box 399,
Summerland, B.C. V0H 1Z0

•••

10

Last Mountain

| Statistics | For map, see page 64. |

Distance:	11.5 km, from Hwy 97 in Westbank.
Travel Time:	One half hour.
Condition:	Paved, with gravel sections.
Season:	Year around. May need chains in winter.
Topo Maps:	Kelowna, B.C. 82 E/14 (1:50,000).
Forest Maps:	Penticton and area.
Communities:	Kelowna, Westbank and Peachland.

Ski Trails and Fishing Lakes

Fig. 10: Jackpine Lake, near Westbank, B.C.

Crystal Mountain ski area (formerly Last Mountain), located 21 kilometres (13 miles) southwest of Kelowna and 11.5 kilometres (seven miles) west of Westbank, is geared to serve the local family-oriented market and it does it well. With only 10 per cent of the ski mountain rated as expert and the remainder evenly divided between beginner and intermediate, its a good place to learn, practice technique or get back in shape to tackle the more demanding Okanagan ski mountains.

With a normal mid-December to late March season, Crystal Mountain offers special rates for afternoon skiing and night skiing. The night skiing is particularly attractive to destination skiers staying in Kelowna and skiing Big White during the day. Spring skiing starts early at Crystal Mountain—why not give it a try this February?

Telemark X-C Ski Trails are also located on Last Mountain. Access from Highway 97 is via Glenrosa Road on the southern outskirts of Westbank, with the large parking area nine kilometres from the highway. Telemark has over 32 kilometres of marked trails, groomed for classic and freestyle skiing. The area also has 2.5 kilometres of lit track for night skiing. Ski fees are reasonable. During the 91/92 season, adult day passes were $6.00 and season passes were $60.00.

Summer can also be an interesting time in the area. You can continue northwest up Powers Creek for another 10 kilometres and then west for five kilometres into Jackpine Lake for a little fishing or camping at a Forest Service Recreation Site. You can also continue farther north and up to Bear F.S. Road for some further back-country exploring. (See the *Bear Road* section starting on page 63 for details.)

•••

Additional Information Sources.

Crystal Mountain,
P.O. Box 97,
Westbank, B.C. V0H 2A0
Tel: (604) 768-5189

•••

11

Hardy Falls Park

Statistics

Distance:	29 km, Kelowna to Hardy Falls Park.
	4 km, Peachland (Princeton Ave) to the park.
Travel Time:	Approximately $\frac{1}{2}$ hour from Kelowna.
Condition:	Paved highway (Highway 97).
Season:	Year-around.
Topo Maps:	Summerland, B.C. 82 E/12 (1:50,000).
Forest Maps:	Penticton and Area.
Communities:	Peachland.

Peachland's Pleasant Getaway

Hardy Falls Park, on Peachland (Deep) Creek in south Peachland, is a cool oasis in what can sometimes be a hot landscape. A pleasant walking trail begins at a parking lot and picnic site on Hardy Street, just off Highway 97 on the southern outskirts of Peachland. The kilometre-long-trail, complete with seven footbridges, leads to a splendid little falls hidden away at the head of a narrow canyon. Allow $\frac{1}{2}$ to 1 hour to make the trip to the falls.

In April, the sunflower-like blossoms of the arrowleaf balsamroot brighten the slopes and the yellow flowers of the Oregon grape add splotches of color to the underbrush. Carp spawn in the creek, while a dipper nests in a crevice part way up the waterfall. In October, the Oregon grape fruit turns a dusty blue and crimson Kokanee dart among the riffles in the creek.

Although the sign is marked "1972", the park had already gone through several incarnations by that date, starting off as an

Order-in-Council setting aside 15.4 hectares (38 acres) in October, 1949. The B.C. Parks Branch established Antlers Beach Park in 1955, taking in Okanagan Lake waterfront and the creek-side property. At the time of writing, the park has been transferred to the Regional District of Central Okanagan.

According to Stella (Gummow) Welch in *Peachland Memories, Volume Two* (pp 379-384), "It was the fall of 1884 that Harry Hardy came down through the Okanagan Valley for the first time, and on New Year's Day, 1885, he got his first glimpse of what was later Peachland, and his home for many years. The pack train that he had was loaded with flour from Lee Pollen's mill at Spallumcheen, and came down the west side of the lake. There were a few settlers, bachelors, in the Valley, and at Trepanier Creek "Wild Goose Bill" —Bill Jenkins— was the only settler on the ranch that was later sold to the Lambly brothers.

"Leaving the lake south of this point, they took the old Allison Trail to what later became Princeton. At that time [John Fall] Allison had a little store and a post office there, and the pack load of flour was sold for twelve dollars for each hundred pound bag, a large amount for that time."

Mrs. Welch continues her narrative. "Leaving the pack train because of deep snow, which made the return trip impossible, Harry Hardy walked to the Tom Ellis place where Penticton is now, stayed there for the night and walked up the east side of the lake to Mission and on to Priest's Valley, now Vernon."

Harry Hardy soon "got a job with Bob Lambly. The Lambly Brothers had bought out the squatter, Bill Jenkins, at Trepanier and pre-empted District Lot 220, and Harry Hardy was sent down to look after the stock. Peachland became his home from that time on and he thus became the first permanent settler."

Irrigating with water from Trepanier Creek, Harry Hardy planted the first peach orchard in the Okanagan Valley in 1885.

"In 1891 Hardy pre-empted land where Gorman's Mill now stands, its southern boundary being *Hardy's Lake*, known to old timers as the *Turtle Ponds*... At this property he planted about 200 fruit trees, one of the first orchards in the Westbank area."

According to Stella Welch, "it would seem he cared for the two properties at the same time.

"The first peaches ripened on the young orchard at Trepanier Creek gave the idea of a new venture to J.M. Robinson, energetic mine promoter. He had earlier induced a number of prairie farmers to invest

Fig. 11: Hardy Falls on Peachland (Deep) Creek.

in mining claims, and a little cluster of homes housed these venturing pioneers. But no ore was ever taken out, and Mr. Robinson's first taste of a delicious peach, which Mr. Hardy declared was nine inches around, opened up a whole new prospect. J.M. Robinson bought up pre-emptions in and around Peachland, paying Harry $600.00 for a pre-emption he had which extended from the lakeshore to the top bench, D.L. 1184. He sub-divided these into ten-acre plots, and went down to Winnipeg to sell them. John Gummow with his young family arrived from Winnipeg in December 1899, and the first orchard planted on the south side of the village came into being. His first crop of huge potatoes grown on this new and fertile land, with the aid of a plowed furrow as an irrigation ditch, inspired the disgruntled miners to buy up land for orchards, and the new settlement took form as a fruit-growing community.

"But," continues Welch, "Harry Hardy, in the meantime, left the Lambly Ranch to do a little prospecting on his own...

"After several disappointing years spent prospecting, Harry Hardy bought ten acres of his own pre-emption back from J.M. Robinson, and started an orchard of his own. This was later sold and Harry spent the last years of his life in his little home in town... He passed on quietly March 21, 1947 at the age of 89 years."

•••

Information Sources

Peachland Memories, Volume Two. Compiled by the Peachland Historical Society, Box 244, Peachland, B.C., V0H 1X0

Additional Information Sources

B.C. Parks
P.O. Box 399,
Summerland, B.C. V0H 1Z0

Regional District of Central Okanagan
540 Groves Avenue,
Kelowna, B.C. V1Y 4Y7
Tel: (604) 763-4918

•••

Headwaters Lakes

Statistics	For map, see page 59.
Distance:	24 km, Sunset Interchange (97C) to Headwaters. 27 km, Headwaters to Hwy 97 in Peachland.)
Travel Time:	Up to one hour on each leg.
Elevation Diff.	1355 metres, Sunset Lake to Peachland.
Condition:	Gravel road with some rough sections.
Season:	Early July to late October.
Topo Maps:	Tulameen, B.C. 92 H/NE (1:100,000). Kelowna, B.C. 82 E/NW (1:100,000).
Forest Maps:	Merritt - Princeton & Penticton and Area.
Communities:	Merritt, Westbank and Peachland.

Floating Islands and Fighting Trout

Ron and Kathleen Farrell made the BIG MOVE a couple of years ago. You know the "big move" I'm writing about—the move we all think about, the move some of us talk about and the move that very few of us actually make. Their move came when Ron was fifty-plus with a job with a Vancouver food wholesaler and Kathy had a senior position in a hospital.

The Farrells left their payroll jobs in the city and bought the Headwaters Fishing Camp, half an hour west of Peachland. They left the rat-race of the "big smoke" and the well-kept lawns of suburbia. They sold what they couldn't take with them and packed up the rest and headed for the hills. Now, the closest they come to a well-kept lawn is when they help an Okanagan Valley friend pick nightcrawlers for their worm farm. And a big smoke is when their guests gets a little carried away with their campfires.

Finding the Farrells and the Headwaters Fishing Camp is a back-roader's delight. In mid-summer, there are at least half a dozen ways to approach the Headwaters Lakes area—the "headwaters" being the upper reaches of Trout Creek in the highlands west of Okanagan Lake. In mid-winter, there is only one way to take a car or truck in and that is from Peachland.

Fig. 12: Sunset Lake, looking east.

Making the Headwaters connection from the Okanagan Connector (Hwy 97C) is no difficult task in mid-summer. Because of the altitude and the snowfall in the Pennask Mountain area, the route may not be open until early July and you could find snow again blocking your way towards the end of October. Leave the Okanagan Connector (Hwy 97C) at the Sunset Main Road interchange (kilometre 0.0) and follow the rough and narrow gravel road east along the south side of the highway. The road improves as you get farther from the freeway.

Fig. 13: Fishermen at MacDonald Lake, west of Peachland.

Your first opportunity for a diversion from dusty driving comes very quickly. Watch for a wide spot on the south side of the road and an unmarked path through the trees at km 1.2. If you're successful at dodging the boulders, you can park here and take a two-minute walk through the lodgepole pine to Sunset Lake. Sunset Lake is not big by any standards. The trail is wide enough to pack in a canoe, but if you didn't bother bringing yours, you can follow the cattle and game trails completely around the lake in less than an hour. There are several rocky outcroppings along the west shore that may provide a vantage point for casting from the shoreline. In the summer of 1991, there were also a few old log rafts beached along this shore. They might not be sea-worthy, but they could give you a bit more room for your back-cast.

If you explore the north end of the lake, you may discover the foundations of at least two small cabins. These were on lease lots that were canceled when the B.C. Parks began steps to create a small roadside park at Sunset Lake. According to one B.C. Parks source, the steps were halted when concern was expressed for the wildlife in the area—but the halt is only expected to be temporary.

After your sojourn to Sunset Lake, continue east along Sunset Main Road (occasionally marked Sunset Lake Forest Road), keeping left at the junction at km 1.8. For reasons that are totally unclear, there was a "STOP" sign at this junction. Follow the main gravel road east to the junction at km 6.5, near the 37K marker. Here a rough road to the left snakes under the freeway next to Pennask Creek. If you are looking for further diversions, you can follow the high voltage power line right-of-way west to Quilchena or Douglas Lake. Check your tires, your fuel and your shovel before you try it—you may find yourself putting all three to the test.

Go straight ahead at the 37K marker and you should cross Pennask Creek and come to the junction of Bear F.S. Road and Sunset Lake Road. To the left lies Pennask Lake and Hatheume Lake, and a long roller-coaster ride down to Okanagan Lake near Bear Creek Provincial Park, opposite Kelowna. (See the *Bear Road* section on page 63.)

Go right on Sunset Lake Road and you'll come to the Brenda Lake junction at km 13.9. If rainbow trout fishing is your pleasure, Brenda Lake lies 2.4 km to the left (northeast) and MacDonald Lake is another kilometre farther along. Both lakes have Forest Service recreation sites. Although it is initially deceiving, the MacDonald Lake site has some excellent camping spots in the trees near the lake. You can continue past MacDonald Lake and wind down to Peachland via the Brenda Mine Road. Rumors suggest that once Brenda is finished with mine reclama-

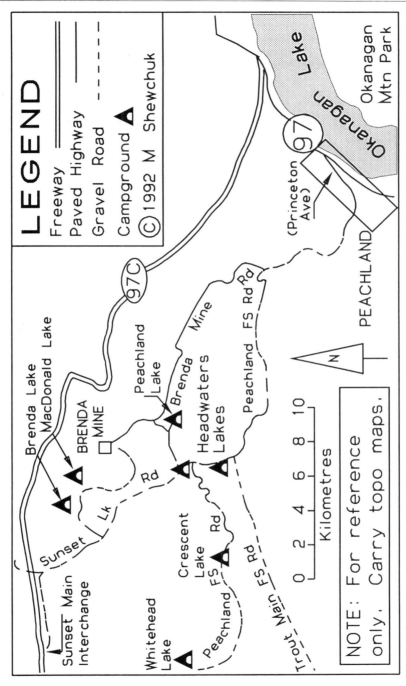

Map 8: Headwaters Lakes area.

tion, you may be able to access the Okanagan Connector at the Brenda Mine interchange.

Fig. 14: A mule deer doe near Headwaters Lake #1.

B ut, as this is the description of the road to the Headwaters Lakes area, back-track to the junction at km 13.9 (near the 31K marker) and follow the road and the "Headwaters" signs southeast. The elevation here is approximately 1,650 metres (5,400 feet) and snow can block your passage until late June. The road skirts the top end of Peachland Creek canyon for about three kilometres before beginning the descent to the Headwaters area. The winding descent—over 400 metres in five kilometres—can be an exciting trip in mud or fresh snow. Watch for logging trucks, particularly on weekdays.

Peachland Lake is only a few minutes off Sunset Lake Road on a side road at km 22, near the 23K signpost. If you still have some swing left in your casting arm, you can detour northeast to Peachland Lake. Like many of the lakes in the region, it is an irrigation reservoir with a fluctuating shoreline and plenty of snags. Spring high water, however, hides a multitude of sins. It's about two kilometres to the lake and a total of four kilometres to a large, open recreation site which has a boat launch and gravel swimming beach—if you want to rinse the dust off your body.

Meanwhile, back at the 23K signpost on Sunset Lake Road. A few hundred metres farther along and you are at the junction of the Peachland F.S. Road and the end (or beginning) of Sunset Lake Road. Hidden in a nearby hollow is Little Loon Lake and across the road, through the trees lies one of the four Headwaters Lakes.

If you want to get away from the crowd, Crescent Lake is 7.5 kilometres and Whitehead Lake is 22 kilometres to the west along the Peachland F.S. Road. The last 2.4 kilometres into Whitehead Lake is rough, but passable for most vehicles in dry weather.

Headwaters Fishing Camp (and the east access to the Headwaters Forest Service rec site) is little more than a kilometre south of the Peachland/Sunset Lake road junction. Ron and Kathy Farrell have owned the fishing camp since the summer of 1989. Before they purchased the property, it belonged to Erik Blondell and Norm Clermont. The ownership lineage goes back through Ned and Donna Rathbun, June and Terry Beamish and others to the granting of the fishing camp's first operating permit in April, 1939. Ron Farrell believes that the original cabin may have been built by a trapper as early as 1928.

This trapper's task may have been to remove the beaver that were a constant source of concern to the Summerland Irrigation District. The district acquired water rights to Trout Creek when it was incorporated in 1906 and built dams on Crescent Lake, Whitehead Lake and the Headwaters Lakes in the 1920s and 30s.

The dams helped create Headwaters Lake No. 1's floating islands. According to Ron Farrell, there are five of them with three quite large. These may have been sections of marsh that broke free when the dams raised the lake levels, but they are now tree-covered chunks of land. It can cause more than a little confusion when you go to sleep looking out over blue water and awaken to see an eagle's nest in a tree directly in front of your camp.

The Farrells offer excellent hospitality and fishing camp basics. They have cabins, campsites, canoes, boats and motors. They also have a hot shower and a small convenience store. But you won't find a restaurant, lounge, pool or sauna.

Headwaters Lake No. 1 has eastern brook trout to 1.5 kilograms (three pounds) and rainbow trout over one kilogram (two pounds), says Ron Farrell. Eastern brook trout were introduced into the lake in the mid 1980s because of a coarse fish problem. "They eat the suckers like mad." says Farrel.

Because of the elevation at Headwaters (1,250 metres or 4,100 feet), the weather is noticeably cooler and the summers shorter than in the Okanagan Valley. Camping is generally from early May until after Thanksgiving.

But backroads exploring doesn't end when the snow flies. The road from Peachland to Headwaters is kept open all winter. Snowmobilers use the old roads to gain access to the surrounding lakes and the 1,995 metre (6,545 foot) peak of nearby Pennask Mountain. Cross-country skiers, including Kathleen Farrell, enjoy the lakes and the easy grades of the local forest roads.

From the entrance to Headwaters Fishing Camp, Peachland Forest Road continues south and then southeast for 25 kilometres before reaching Highway 97 in Peachland. Your first opportunity for a detour is at the Trout Main F.S. Road junction at km 25, a bit over a kilometre south of the camp entrance. The Princeton-Summerland Road lies 20 kilometres to the south over a generally good gravel road that follows Trout Creek toward Summerland. (See *Osprey Lakes Road*, page 79 for details.)

If you stay on the gravel road to Peachland, you will follow Greata Creek down to Peachland Creek, reaching the Brenda Mine Road at km 39, about 15 kilometres from Headwaters. Silver Lake Camp is located four kilometres to the west and Peachland and the shores of Okanagan Lake lie another 12 kilometres to the east.

If you've chosen to make the trip on a warm summer day, you will definitely notice the temperature change from 1,700 metre (5,600 foot) Sunset Lake to 341 metre (1,120 foot) Okanagan Lake—and you will quickly learn why the deer head for the uplands in summer.

●●●

Additional Information Sources:

Ron & Kathleen Farrell
Headwaters Fishing Camp
Box 350, Peachland, B.C. V0H 1X0
Tel: 604 767-2400

●●●

13

Bear Road

Statistics   **For map, see page 64.**

Distance:	69 km, Okanagan Connector to Westside Road.
Travel Time:	Two to three hours.
Elevation Diff.	1300 metres, Pennask Lake to Okanagan Lake.
Condition:	Rough gravel, may be closed in winter.
Season:	July through October.
Topo Maps:	Tulameen, B.C. 92 H/NE (1:100,000).
	Kelowna, B.C. 82 E/NW (1:100,000).
Forest Maps:	Penticton and Area.
Communities:	Peachland, Westbank and Kelowna.

Upland Lakes and Mountain Backroads

Bear Road begins (or ends, depending on your direction of travel) at its junction with Sunset Main Road near the Pennask Creek overpass on the Okanagan Connector. Although the junction is within sight of the freeway, the nearest access to the Connector (Highway 97C) is at the Sunset Main Road interchange approximately 6.5 kilometres to the west. (See *Headwaters Lakes*, page 55 for details.) The elevation of this part of the Interior Plateau is about 1,600 metres (5,250 feet) so the road may not be passable until mid or late June. But when it is open, it is a pleasant, though sometimes bumpy, alternative to the freeway—an alternative that allows access to several Forest Service recreation sites and some of the finest trout lakes in the B.C. Interior.

With the Bear Road—Sunset Main Road junction as kilometre 0.0, head north toward the Okanagan Connector and drive under it at km 0.4, keeping right on Bear F.S. Road at a junction near km 2.8. The next major junction at km 7.2 (near the 43K tag) marks Pennask F.S. Road and the private access to Pennask Lake Lodge.

63

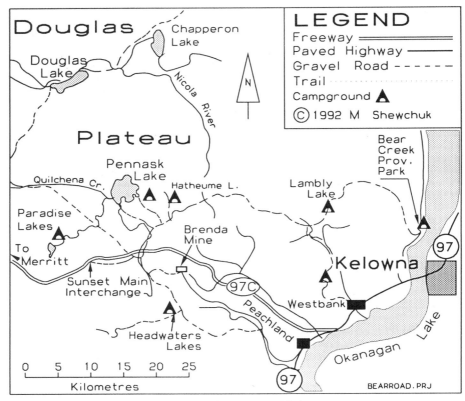

Map 9: Sunset Lake to Kelowna.

James D. Dole, whose name is synonymous with Hawaiian pine-apple, first visited Pennask Lake in September, 1927. Accompanied by his wife, Belle, two employees, and three friends who then managed the lodge at Fish Lake (Lac Le Jeune) near Kamloops, Dole camped for a week at the head of Pennask Lake.

In the book, *A Place Called Pennask,* Stanley E. Read writes that James Dole was in search of a dream—to be part of a fishing club that could control its surroundings. He wanted a lake of perfect fishing in a region teeming with attractions which he and his friends could call their own. He found it in Pennask Lake and moved quickly to gain control.

In a memorandum dated October 26, 1928, Dole wrote, "We believe that by controlling the land at shore-front we can maintain good fishing in this lake for a long time to come, and it is hoped that it will be kept as a fly-fishing lake solely and not be dredged... with tin shops and worms."

64

Fig. 15: Canoeing on Pennask Lake.

The Pennask Lake Club was established in 1929, and officially incorporated in June, 1930, as the Pennask Lake Company, Ltd. Membership was to be limited to 50 at a fee of $1,000 per member. Several prominent U.S. citizens joined the club, but the Great Depression dealt a series of setbacks before Dole's plans could materialize. The new lodge was under-utilized, resulting in deficits that Dole made up from his personal finances. It was not until the late 1940s, when the Pennask Lake Fishing and Game Club was formed, that new financial life was breathed into the operation—under Canadian control.

In 1970, Pennask Lake was formally established as a "fly-fishing-only" lake. Pennask Lake continues to be an important source of Rainbow trout eggs for the provincial stocking program.

While access is restricted at the lodge, the junction to Pennask Lake Park is about half a kilometre farther along Bear Road. This site, on the southeast corner of the lake, is about six kilometres off the main forest access road. The public area was first established as a Class A Park on May 2, 1974, but was downgraded to a Recreational Area early in 1975. There were several reasons for the change: the new status would allow ranching interests to keep their cattle in the area; limited resource development would be allowed if it would not damage recreational values; but probably most important of all, it would limit park development and consequent pressures on Pennask Lake as the province's most important source of rainbow trout eggs. While facilities are still limited, the recreation area was recently upgraded to a park.

The construction of Coquihalla Highway Phase III—now known as the Okanagan Connector—prompted some major soul-searching on the part of B.C. Parks. The present rough access road limits the number of visitors to the recreation site, but with a major highway only a short distance away, pressure will certainly be felt to improve access and facilities at the lake.

At km 12.2, about 4.5 kilometres north of the junction to Pennask Lake Recreation Area, another side-road leads 4.3 kilometres northwest to Pinnacle Lake and Hatheume Lake. Although Hatheume Lake is considerably smaller than Pennask, it too has a widespread reputation as a source of fighting rainbow trout. At the time of writing, Hatheume was a catch-and-release fishery with a further restriction of barbless hooks. There is a medium-sized Forest Service recreation site on the south side of Hatheume Lake and a resort on the northeast shore.

From the junction to Pennask Lake Park, Bear Road scribes a wide arc as it descends to Okanagan Lake. First it continues on a generally easterly direction, passing Windy Lake (with a small Forest Service rec site) before joining a better road near Cameo Lake. The Cameo Lake rec site, at km 28.6, is one of the busiest in the region. From Cameo Lake, the road continues eastward, crossing the height of land between Lacoma Creek and Powers Creek and dropping again into the Lambly Creek drainage.

Jackpine Forest Service Road, at km 41.6, winds down through the Powers Creek valley to Westbank, passing side roads into Jackpine Lake and the Crystal Mountain ski area. (See page 49.)

Lambly (Bear) Lake, at km 45, has a Forest Service rec site and a place to launch your boat on this reservoir lake.

L ambly Lake takes its name from the Lambly brothers, a trio of pioneer settlers who came to the Okanagan Valley in the 1870s. According to an article in *Peachland Memories, Volume Two*, (pp. 426-430) the Lamblys were natives of Megantic County, Quebec, an area settled by United Empire Loyalists.

Robert Lambly, the first to arrive in the Okanagan, tramped in from the coast over the Hope Trail and initially settled in what is now the Enderby district. A year later he was joined by his brother Thomas who took up land nearby.

Charles Lambly followed his brothers westward in 1878 and obtained work as a civil engineer in northern British Columbia. A decade later, Charles moved into the Enderby area to work on the construction of the Shuswap and Okanagan Railway. Charles soon entered the service of the Provincial Government, first as Assessor, and later as Mining Recorder, Gold Commissioner, Stipendiary Magistrate and still later, Government Agent. His first post was Enderby, as the young town at "Lambly's Landing" was christened, but soon he was off to Rock Creek, where he spent the rest of his life.

The other Lambly brothers, Thomas and Robert, continued to live in the Enderby area until 1894. Some years earlier they had acquired land on the west side of Okanagan Lake at Trepanier Creek, with extensive range north and west of present day Peachland. (See *Hardy Falls Park*, page 51.)

The brothers had bought out William Jenkins who had located at Trepanier Creek in 1886, and on March 1, 1887 a pre-emption for D.L. 220 was registered to Charles A.R. Lambly, the first pre-emption in the district. Charles also purchased D.L. 490 in 1893, and his brother, Tom, bought D.L. 449 the same year. These properties all fronted on Okanagan Lake, and gave the brothers five kilometres of lakeshore. On the lakeside property at Trepanier they experimented with fruit growing, and pioneered the growing of soft fruits in that area.

"This was not the brothers only activity in the area," states the article in *Peachland Memories*. "While ranging the horses and cattle on the hills they had done some prospecting, and had become the possessors of a number of likely-looking mining claims.

"This unfortunately led to a tragedy.

"Tom Lambly contracted a severe cold while doing some development work on claims west of Trepanier. This turned into pneumonia and he was taken across the lake to Kelowna for treatment, but to no avail, and he died there on Nov. 24, 1897."

Following the death of his brother, Robert Lambly moved back to Enderby to reside, after disposing of part of the Trepanier holdings. A short time later he moved with his wife and family to Alberta, where he operated a stock ranch in the foothills of the Rockies.

The road across the upper elevations of the plateau is sometimes rough and slow-going. But beyond Lambly (Bear) Lake, Bear Road is well maintained on the 25-kilometre descent to the pavement at Westside Road. On one trip through the area, we noted motorcycle racing taking place in the grasslands near km 58. And on a future trip, we hope to explore Bald Range Road, km 61.5, into the Terrace Mountain area.

Bear Road joins Westside Road approximately 69 kilometres from its start near the Okanagan Connector underpass and approximately 8.5 kilometres north of the junction of Westside Road and Highway 97. If you are looking for a place to camp for the night, you may want to consider Bear Creek Provincial Park, at the mouth of Lambly Creek.

•••

Additional Information Sources

A Place Called Pennask, by Stanley E. Read (1977), Mitchell Press.
Cattle Ranch, The Story of the Douglas Lake Cattle Company, by Nina G. Woolliams (1979), published by Douglas & McIntyre.
Peachland Memories, Volume Two. (1983) Published by the Peachland Historical Society, Box 244, Peachiand, B.C., V0H 1X0

B.C. Parks
P.O. Box 399,
Summerland, B.C. V0H 1Z0

•••

14

South Okanagan: An Overview
Similkameen/South Okanagan/Boundary

Fig. 16: Beach at Christie Memorial Park, Skaha Lake.

The South Okanagan, Similkameen and Boundary districts of British Columbia have many similarities and many differences. At the lower elevations, the climate of all three is generally hot and dry in summer and moderate and dry in winter. Without the irrigation water that is pumped from the rivers or captured in the hills, the bottomland would be as dry and barren as the nearby sage-covered hillsides.

69

But it isn't dry and barren—and that is one of the important attractions of the region. Where sprinklers cast their man-made rainbows, a virtual Garden of Eden flourishes. Cherries, apricots, peaches and plums are harvested as the summer progresses. Apples and pears are cultivated in many varieties and follow the soft fruit harvest. Grapes—raw material for the wine-making industry—grow on the slopes, row upon row. The Boundary district may not have quite the variety, but it does provide a rich harvest of fruit, vegetables and livestock. Add juicy berries and you have the stock for one of Canada's largest concentrations of roadside fruitstands.

What healthier form of recreation is there than fruitstand shopping?

Once you've filled your basket, you can head for the beaches of Okanagan, Skaha or Osoyoos lakes—or one of the dozen other lakes on the valley floor or the nearby hills. You can practice your swing at one of many golf courses, ride an inner tube down the Okanagan or Similkameen rivers, or bird watch in the riverside oxbows or sagebrush-covered hills near Osoyoos Lake. If you are really serious about hills, you can explore Apex Mountain Recreational Area, Nickel Plate Park, Cathedral Park or the south slopes of Okanagan Mountain Park and bring back fine memories of the mountains.

If you choose not to hibernate in winter, the alpine again beckons. Strap on the slats and try alpine skiing at Mount Baldy or Apex. If speed's not your forte, the cross-country ski trail networks at Mount Baldy, Apex or Nickel Plate are sure to help keep you fit.

After a day on the trails or at the beach, the cities beckon. Penticton, the south Okanagan's *Hospitality Capital of Canada* has many fine restaurants, an excellent Library/Museum centre, and tempting beaches at both ends. You can even try your hand (or legs) at bungy-jumping.

Osoyoos also has its beaches, and a Spanish theme to go with the nearby pocket desert. With plenty of restaurants, stores and fruitstands, starvation shouldn't be a problem. Oliver is set halfway between Vaseux Lake and Osoyoos Lake, with the beach at little Tuc-Ul-Nuit Lake competing with the best.

Over Richter Pass to the west lies Canada's Similkameen country. I may be wrong, but I suspect that Keremeos has more fruitstands per kilometre than any other place in Canada—and at least one of them is open year-around. Over Anarchist Mountain, to the east of the Okanagan, lies the Boundary District—and Doukhobor country. This narrow stretch of land has a heritage as rich as any in Canada.

The choices are many—and they're all yours.

•••

15

Okanagan Lake Park

Statistics

Distance:	25 km, Penticton to Okanagan Lake Park.
	35 km, Kelowna to Okanagan Lake Park.
Condition:	Paved highway, some four-lane sections.
Season:	Year around, north park closed in winter.
Topo Maps:	Summerland, B.C. 82 E/12 (1:50,000).
	Kelowna, B.C. 82 E/NW (1:100,000).
Forest Maps:	Penticton and Area.
Communities:	Summerland, Peachland & Westbank.

Camping and more, by Okanagan Lake

Okanagan Lake Provincial Park is situated along the western shores of Okanagan Lake, a short drive north of Summerland and approximately 25 kilometres north of Penticton. Highway 97, continuing north to Kelowna and Vernon, passes directly through the park, dividing the terraced, developed campground sections below from the rocky hills above. The upper sections of the park typify the dry, semi-desert landscape for which the Okanagan Valley is famous.

Founded in 1955, Okanagan Lake Provincial Park is an example of park planning with the intent to create an area with a striking contrast to the native vegetation. In the latter part of the same decade, the first of over 10,000 trees were planted in the foreshore area of the park. Today you can set up your camp in the shade of any one of a dozen exotic trees, including Manitoba, silver and Norway maples, Russian olive, Chinese elm, Lombardy poplar, and red, blue and mountain ashes. In the hills above, natural stands of ponderosa pine and Douglas fir continue to share the rocky landscape with sagebrush, bunchgrass, and cacti, as they have for centuries.

Fig. 17: A robin eyes the photographer from a poplar.

Fig. 18: A nearly-deserted beach in the morning light.

The extensive tree cover provides a haven for a tremendous variety of bird life. Many species, including cedar waxwing, quail, red-shafted flicker, western meadow lark, Lewis woodpecker, and several varieties of hummingbirds can be spotted here with little difficulty. Along the many hiking trails in the dry upland areas of the park, you might well come across a harmless gopher snake sunning itself quietly on a rocky outcrop, or a colony of Columbian groundsquirrels eyeing you suspiciously from the safety of their burrows.

The park's recreational activities focus on the warm, clear waters of Okanagan Lake. There is more than a kilometre of sandy beaches, and the opportunities for windsurfers, swimmers, sailors, fishermen, water-skiers, picnickers, and sun worshipers are virtually limitless. Okanagan Lake Park is unusual in that it consists of two campgrounds instead of one. The park has a total of 160 vehicle/tent campsites, 84 in the north campground, and another 76 in the south campground. There are day use/picnic areas in both campgrounds, as well as changehouses, showers, pit and flush toilets, boat ramps, and a sani-station. Interpretive programs are provided from the end of June until the Labour Day weekend.

Because of the park's tremendous popularity during the busy summer months, a number system has been instituted to ensure a fair and equitable method of providing available campsites on a first come, first served basis. As is the case in many B.C. provincial parks, Okanagan Lake has a campground host/hostess resident in the park to answer all of your questions and make your stay a pleasant and memorable one.

The boat ramp at Okanagan Lake Provincial Park is also a departure point for the marine campgrounds and trails on the west slopes of 10,000 hectares (25,000 acres) Okanagan Mountain Provincial Park. It is also accessible by road from either Kelowna or Penticton. (See the *Okanagan Mountain Park* section, page 21, for details.)

• • •

Additional Information Sources:

B.C. Parks
P.O. Box 399,
Summerland, B.C.
V0H 1Z0

Summerland Chamber of
Commerce,
Box 1075, Highway 97,
Summerland, B.C. V0H 1Z0

• • •

Giant's Head Mountain

Statistics	For map, see page 78.
Distance:	Approximately 5 km, Hwy 97 to summit.
Travel Time:	Allow 1 to 2 hours, including hike to top.
Elevation Gain:	500 metres.
Condition:	Mostly paved, very narrow and steep.
Season:	Best in dry weather.
Topo Maps:	Summerland, B.C. 82 E/12 (1:50,000).
Forest Maps:	Penticton and Area.
Communities:	Summerland.

A Top with a View

One of the finest viewpoints in the south Okanagan is situated in the heart of Summerland. Giant's Head Mountain, with a 360 degree perspective from 500 metres (1,640 feet) above Okanagan Lake, is the ideal point to get a true appreciation of the lay of the land.

Getting to the peak is relatively simple. If you are traveling along Highway 97 in upper Summerland, turn west on Prairie Valley Road, then south on Atkinson Road to Giant's Head Road. After a very short jaunt on Giant's Head Road, make a sharp turn to the right and head west on Milne Road. Watch for the signs and the stone gateway marking the start of the narrow switchback road to the picnic site near the top. Cars and smaller trucks should have little difficulty in dry weather, but leave your motorhomes, campers and holiday trailers at the parking area near the gate. From the parking area and picnic site near the top, several trails crisscross the ridge. The main route goes south and up with a switchback walking trail and a straighter route that has been gouged out of the mountain by errant 4x4s or ATVs.

Fig. 19: Summerland from Giant's Head Mountain.

Markers clearly point out many of the local landmarks. Across the lake to the northeast is Okanagan Mountain and Okanagan Mountain Provincial Park. Across the lake to the east is Naramata, with several fine beaches. If you look carefully to the northeast, you may be able to pick out the twisting path of the Kettle Valley Railroad as it descends from Chute Lake on its way to Penticton. Just below you to the south is the community of Trout Creek and the Summerland Agricultural Research Station. Okanagan Lake, Skaha Lake and Vaseux Lake lie progressively farther south. Nearer to the south and southwest, you should be able to pick out the meandering path of the Kettle Valley Railway as it begins its steady climb out of the Okanagan Valley on its way to Princeton. With the Summerland, B.C. (82 E/12) topographic map as a reference, you may be able to visually follow Prairie Valley Road as it heads up Trout Creek and then cross-country to Princeton.

I f map reading doesn't enthrall you, you may be interested in the excellent variety of dry-country wildflowers and shrubs that cling to the mountain slopes. Yellow avalanche lilies and arrowleaf balsamroot dominate the scene in April and May, but a closer look will reveal shooting stars, scarlet gilia and a host of other plant species. Saskatoon bushes thrust forth their white blossoms before most other plants bear any leaves, showing clumps of white on a drab brown slope. By early summer, the purple fruit attracts birds, chipmunks and anyone interested in a little variety in their berry pies.

• • •

Fig. 20: Sighting tubes help distinguish local landmarks.

Additional Information Sources

Summerland Chamber of Commerce
Box 1075,
Summerland, B.C. V0H 1Z0

• • •

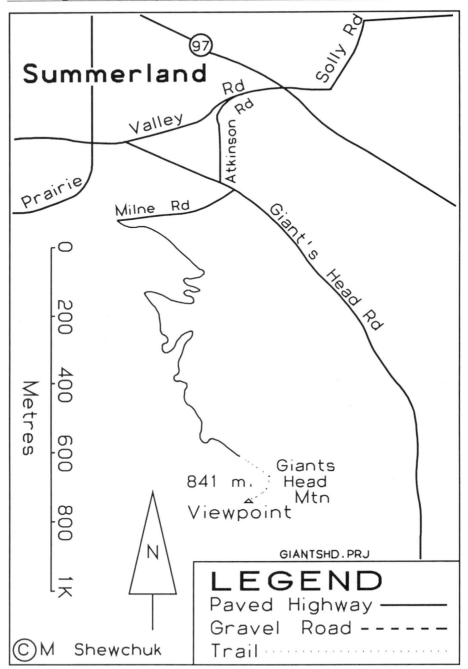

Map 10: Giant's Head Park and downtown Summerland.

17

Osprey Lakes Road

Statistics   For map, see page 81.

Distance: 95 km, Summerland to Princeton.
Travel Time: Two to three hours.
Elevation Gain: 860 metres.
Condition: Mixed paved and gravel sections.
Season: Best in the dry months.
Topo Maps: Kelowna, B.C. 82 E/NW (1:100,000).
                  Tulameen, B.C. 92 H/NE (1:100,000).
                  Princeton, B.C. 92 H/SE (1:100,000).
Communities: Summerland and Princeton.

The Backroad to Princeton

Visit the Sumac Ridge winery, stock up at the local fruitstands, fill up with gasoline and groceries and prepare to head for the hills in search of some fine trout lakes, hidden Forest Service recreation sites and the last remnants of the famous Kettle Valley Railway.

The Osprey Lakes Road (Princeton-Summerland Road) follows much the same route across this section of the Interior Plateau as the former Kettle Valley Railway. Labeled "Prairie Valley Road" in Summerland, the eastern end of this upland backroad begins at a set of traffic lights on Highway 97 in upper Summerland. This backroad is paved for the first 11 kilometres and the last 45 kilometres, with some rough gravel sections in the Trout Creek canyon area.

With the junction of Prairie Valley Road and Highway 97 as your kilometre 0.0 reference, follow the road as it winds through the village and out into an orchard-covered prairie that certainly isn't obvious from the main highway. Watch for the signs marked "Osprey Lakes" or "Fish Lake" as you climb into the dry hills above Summerland.

Fig. 21: Fisherman and dog on Chain Lake.

Bald Range Road, at km 11.0, is your first major junction. The road to the left continues up into the highlands, gradually getting narrower and rougher as it passes Darke Lake (Fish Lake). Bald Range Road, to the right, climbs away from the valley and up to a narrow bench high above Trout Creek. This is the truly scenic route to the Osprey Lakes and Princeton, and for the next 10 kilometres it offers several spectacular views of the Trout Creek Canyon and the arid rangeland. Wildflowers dominate the slopes in late April and May, but by July everything has a distinctive brown look about it.

Brown gives way to green as the road crosses Trout Creek, near km 25.0, at the bottom of the Trout Creek valley. Forest Service campgrounds (basically a table or two and a biffy) have been established at several places along the creek for the fisherman, hunter and itinerant tourist. The only service provided is the space among the trees. Carry in drinking water, fuel and supplies and carry out any garbage. These campsites do have their advantages, for even in mid-summer

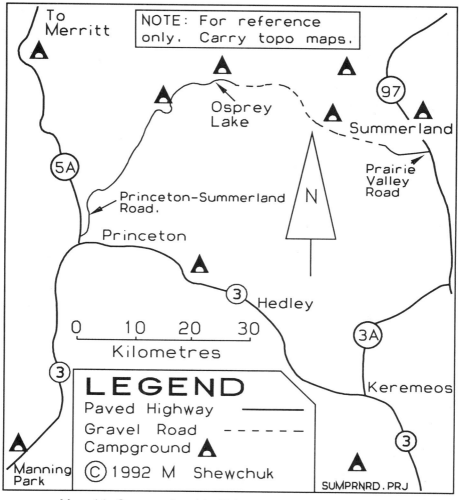

NOTE: For reference only. Carry topo maps.

Map 11: Summerland to Princeton via Osprey Lake.

quiet solitude can be had with the only sounds being the yodel of a not-too-distant coyote and the gurgle of the stream.

A minute's drive beyond the Trout Creek bridge, the road crosses the railbed of the former Kettle Valley Railway. The last train ran over the section from Spences Bridge to Okanagan Falls in May, 1989, and the twin steel rails are being (or have been) removed. A Rails-to-Trails group has lobbied to have portions of the old right-of-way set aside for recreational purposes, but at the time of writing discussions were still under way.

81

Thirsk Lake, at km 42, serves as a reservoir for the orchards in the Summerland area, storing precious water for the hot summer months. Lake levels fluctuate significantly during the irrigation season as the water that begins in the Headwaters Lakes area is metered out via Trout Creek.

Osprey Lake, (at km 51) Link Lake and Chain Lake form the popular Osprey Lakes chain near the summit of this backroad. Fishing is fine throughout most of the summer because of the altitude. Driving conditions also improve considerably as the rest of the road to Princeton is now paved.

Switchback or hairpin turns are common on mountain roads, but not nearly so common on railways. After seriously considering a number of alternative routes to Princeton, Kettle Valley Railway (KVR) Chief Engineer Andrew McCulloch used the undulating grasslands to his advantage when he designed the line's descent into the Allison Creek Valley north of Princeton. From the Separation Lakes area, near km 87, the railway line makes four wide loops down the hillside as it follows Belfort Creek to the valley floor. The road crosses the railway right-of-way several times, offering glimpses of the switchback loops between the low rolling hills.

Osprey Lakes Road, here labeled the Princeton-Summerland Road, joins the Old Hedley Road and Highway 5A on the northern outskirts of Princeton, near km 94. Directly across the highway, another side road leads to the old mining towns of Coalmont and Tulameen and Otter Lake Provincial Park, but that's another trip.

Princeton, a community of 4,000 at the junction of Highway 5A and 3, at km 95, is the gateway to the dry interior for those traveling east on the Crowsnest Route. It was once known as Vermilion Forks because of the red ochre deposits nearby. More on the history of the region can be obtained from the museum and archives on Vermilion Avenue, near the Princeton city centre.

•••

Additional Information Sources:

Summerland Chamber of Commerce
Box 1075,
Summerland, B.C. V0H 1Z0

•••

18

Nickel Plate Road

Statistics   For map, see page 85.

Distance:	60 km, Penticton to Highway 3 near Hedley.
Travel Time:	One to two hours.
Elevation Gain:	1,640 metres.
Condition:	Partly paved; some rough gravel sections.
Season:	Nickel Plate to Hedley may be closed in winter.
Topo Maps:	Penticton, B.C. 82E/SW (1:100,000).
	Kelowna, B.C. 82E/NW (1:100,000).
	Princeton, B.C. 92H/SE (1:100,000).
Communities:	Penticton, Keremeos and Hedley.

Skiing, Fishing and a Gold Mine

The backroad from Penticton to Hedley via Nickel Plate Mountain has intrigued me for two decades. The switchback road up from the Similkameen Valley near Hedley always struck me as one best suited to a mountain goat, not a vehicle. A 1970s Rockhound Rendezvous in the Keremeos-Hedley area introduced me to the waste piles of the old mines on the mountain. And although I succeeded in finding my way up the road and a boulder with a few flakes of silver, it was several years before I was able to drive right through the area which I had learned so much about from prospectors and old B.C. Mines Reports.

In order to take advantage of Forest Service kilometre markers and still provide a guide for the complete trip from Penticton to Hedley via Apex and Nickel Plate, this description is broken into three parts. The first takes in part of the Green Mountain Road from Penticton to the junction to Apex Alpine Ski Resort. The second part covers the route to the ski resort, and the remainder describes the route from Apex past the Nickel Plate Mine to Hedley.

Green Mountain Road suffers from an identity problem, for it is called Fairview Road when it heads east off Channel Parkway, the Highway 97 bypass, in the heart of Penticton's riverside industrial area. For the sake of this book, the junction with Channel Parkway is considered to be kilometre 0.0. The first dozen kilometres of this paved road pass through Penticton Indian Reserve with the opportunity for backroads exploring to Farleigh Lake.

Marron Valley Road, at km 12.6, provides an alternate route to Highway 3A north of the Twin Lakes golf course, but at the time of writing, it was posted with "No Trespassing" signs. The term "marron" has French connections dating back to the fur brigade days. One of its meanings refers to "fugitive" or "wild" and could be related to the wild horses that once roamed the valley. But another meaning is related to chestnut which could also refer to a horse or the reddish-brown fall colors of the surrounding semi-desert hills. Word relationships such as this make the study of place names an interesting, but inexact science.

Marron Valley Road passes the T6 Ranch, then follows a switchback route up the hillside until it overlooks Aeneas Lake near km 5.0. From this midpoint, it follows a route apparently surveyed by the ubiquitous sidehill gouger until it joins Highway 3A approximately 11 kilometres southeast of Green Mountain Road.

It was near the junction of Green Mountain Road and the road to Apex Alpine Ski Resort, km 19.8, that the first Green Mountain House was built. Ezra Mills, the master carpenter of Keremeos, built this roadside stopping-house for Leonard Albert Clark. L.A. Clark was born in Vermont in 1840, and after a stint in the American Civil War on the side of the north, he began a westward trek. He married in Iowa, learned irrigation lay-out in Colorado, railroad grading in Washington state and had a livery stable in Northport, Washington. By 1893, Clark and family were living in Calgary, Alberta, where he installed an irrigation system. He later continued in the same line of work for the Coldstream Orchards at Vernon, B.C.

After trying his luck in the Klondike in 1898, he returned to the Okanagan where he was contracted by M.K. Rodgers of the Nickel Plate Mine to build a road from Penticton to the mine. Clark and his crew began work August 10, 1900. Leonard Clark faced one of the toughest challenges of his varied career as he surveyed feverishly to keep ahead of the construction equipment, but he completed the rough wagon road by that Christmas.

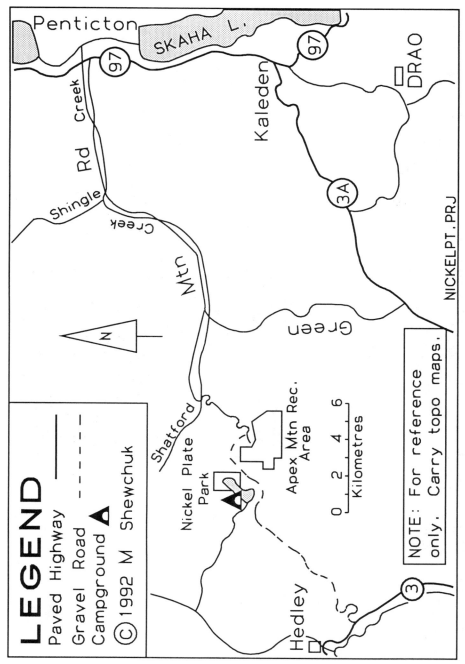

Map 12: Penticton -- Apex Alpine -- Hedley.

Fig. 22: Cross country skiing in the high country.

His route left Penticton and wound up the sand hills on the south side of Shingle Creek, joining the present route of Green Mountain Road about eight kilometres from the Catholic Church on the Indian Reserve. From that point to the mine, nearly 50 kilometres, the route has changed little—a credit to Clark and his crew with their horse-drawn slip scrapers, hand tools, drill steel and blasting powder.

Clark recognized the potential of the area, and with his son Garry, pre-empted about 400 hectares (1,000 acres) of land in the Green Mountain District, named by him after his boyhood Green Mountains of Vermont. Green Mountain House thrived with the steady traffic of freight wagons to and from the mine and the thrice-weekly stage run over the soon-opened road to Olalla and points west in the Similkameen Valley.

When efforts began to develop the Apex Alpine Ski Resort in 1960, the original road to Beaconsfield Mountain (near Apex Mountain) proved woefully inadequate and a new road was started. Mostly single-lane at first, the road has been steadily improved by the Ministry of Highways until today the road to the ski resort is two-lane and paved.

The junction of the Green Mountain Road and the road to Apex, 21 kilometres southwest of Penticton, serves as the km 0.0 reference for the mid-section of this route. From the junction, the road climbs steadily toward the Apex ski area, passing Shatford Road near km 4.0. (Shatford Road winds north then northwest, providing access to the Sheep Rock trail head near km 6.3 and the Mt. Brent trail head near km 9.0.) At first the timber is scattered, but fir and lodgepole pine soon dominate the view.

Apex Village is reached at km 11.5 and the junction to the Hedley-Nickel Plate F.S. Road is well marked at km 13.0. Apex Alpine Ski Resort initially developed the reputation of being on a challenging, technical mountain. The first view of the ski runs from the day lodge still does little to allay the beginner's fears, but a triple chair installed nearly a decade ago opened several excellent beginner and intermediate runs. Now with a mix of about 20 percent beginner, 50 per cent intermediate and 30 per cent advanced runs, the hill appeals to the recreational skier without taking away the challenge that the serious racer enjoyed. For the cross-country skier, ski clubs and the Forest Service maintain an extensive network of trails in the surrounding area.

Apex is the biggest and busiest ski resort in the south Okanagan. It appeals to local skiers as well as visitors determined to sample B.C. Interior sunshine and snow. On-hill condominium accommodations will comfortably handle 450 people, while the resort city of Penticton—half an hour away—can sleep thousands.

Penticton is well-served by bus and air transportation and buses run regularly between the city and the ski resort. On-hill facilities include a wide range of child services including baby-sitting for pre-skiers and a ski school for the junior set. Adults can also sign up for coaching to improve their technique. Apres-ski facilities include a teen centre, restaurants, lounges and outdoor hot tubs next door to the Gunbarrel Saloon.

Hedley-Nickel Plate F.S. Road begins in the upper levels of the Apex village (reset your reference to kilometre 0.0) and passes through an area marked for X-C skiers and snowmobiles at km 2.0. The Hedley Creek-Nickel Plate F.S. Road detours to the right, near the height-of-land and although it is very rough and boulder-strewn, it can be followed west to Nickel Plate Provincial Park on the north shore of Nickel Plate Lake. To get to the park beach, drive or walk west for about 2.6 kilometres and then turn south at a huge boulder. It's less than a kilometre from the boulder to the lake, but unless you are driving an ATV or a 4x4 with exceptional clearance, it is probably safest to park near the boulder and walk the rest of the way. The lake is at an altitude of 1,900 metres (6,230 feet) so the fishing should stay good even during the summer while the swimming is likely to be a bit on the chilly side.

A junction at km 5.0 offers a few options for hiking or backroads exploring. A road to the left follows the power line right-of-way east toward the ski resort for less than a kilometre then branches south to Apex Mountain. Depending on the state of the road and your vehicle, you can drive part of the way and walk the remaining distance to the peak of 2,247 metre high (7,372 feet) Apex Mountain. The total distance is about four to five kilometres, so take drinking water, a lunch and plenty of time.

Another forest road straight ahead at km 5.0, though well used at the time of writing, leads to a maze of logging roads with, as we discovered one late September afternoon, no obvious exit. The Nickel Plate Mine Road to the right has been variously marked by a "Mascot Gold" or "Corona Corporation" sign, but the best reference is the electric power line that leads to the open-pit mine site.

Nickel Plate Nordic Centre, less than a kilometre down the gradual descent, is the focal point of a 25-kilometre network of groomed and track-set cross-country ski trails—with more on the way. An additional 20 kilometres of back country ski trails are accessible from the Nordic Centre. A fine log building serves as a rendezvous and a warming hut for this relatively new operation. Work first started here in May, 1989, and by fall, the trail clearing was well underway. Sale of the logs removed from the trail system helped finance the grooming and the cabin. The system opened in February, 1990, in time for the Penticton Winter Games. The operation still needs funds and volunteers to continue expansion and maintenance. If you can help, contact the Nickel Plate Cross-Country Ski Club, P.O. Box 27, Penticton, B.C. V2A 6J9.

Nickel Plate Lake F.S. Recreation Site is less than two kilometres north of the junction near a creek crossing at km 7.0. Although not as attractive as the park at the north end of the lake, access is much easier for some excellent fly-fishing. The Nickel Plate Road, keeping left, follows Cahill Creek southwest, descending across a lightly-timbered mountain before reaching the open-pit Mascot gold mine at km 12.5.

The operation here is not a new discovery. In fact, the Nickel Plate Mine, 1,200 metres (4,000 feet) above Hedley, was one of B.C.'s first successful hardrock mining operations. Except for a few short breaks, it operated steadily from 1904 to 1956.

From 1900 to late 1909, when the Great Northern Railway reached Hedley, four-horse teams plied the Nickel Plate Road in regular procession, hauling heavy mining and milling equipment from Penticton to Nickel Plate. Once the mine began producing, the teams did not return to Penticton empty.

According to Geoffrey Taylor in *Mining* (Hancock House 1978): "Every month two gold bricks came down to Penticton under special guard and were sent by Dominion Express to Seattle. Concentrates were sacked and hauled by horse-drawn wagon at $9 per ton to Penticton and from there by rail to the smelter in Tacoma. On the return journey the wagons would bring back supplies to Hedley at a contract rate of $20 per ton. The round trip usually took about a week."

The history of the Hedley Mascot operation also goes back to the turn of the century when the Mascot fraction, a triangular claim in the heart of the Nickel Plate orebody, was staked. The owners of the Nickel Plate mine were never able to come to suitable terms with Duncan Wood, owner of the Mascot fraction. In 1934, Hedley Mascot Gold Mines was formed to exploit the Mascot claim and neighboring claims. The ore contained a variety of minerals. For instance, in 1941, 22,477 ounces of gold, 2,755 ounces of silver, 1,300,000 pounds of copper and 2,250,000 pounds of arsenic were produced. In the half century of their first life, the mines on Nickel Plate Mountain produced one and one-half million ounces of gold and four million pounds of copper, worth a total of almost $50 million at the time of production.

To this point, the backroad has been descending steadily from near the Apex ski resort, but after passing the mining operation, it begins to take the process seriously. At first, the timber hides the steepness of the slope, but then the open hillside, dotted with aspen groves, makes the narrow, sometimes muddy switchback descent much more obvious.

A cattleguard and fence at km 21.0 marks a good spot to pull off the road, park and hike to the lip of a nearby rock bluff for an excellent view of the Similkameen Valley, both to the east and west. Caution is advised as there are no guard rails and a fall from the bluff means certain death.

Just beyond the viewpoint area, the road passes through a narrow rock cut and across a section of cliff face that is likely to convince even the bravest backroader to slow down. Once past the cliff, the road continues a steady switchback descent across a slope covered with sagebrush and bunchgrass. Visibility is good—and needed because the narrow road offers few places to safely pass oncoming vehicles. The Nickel Plate Road ends at Highway 3, 26 kilometres from the Apex Alpine Ski Resort and 60 kilometres from Penticton. If you're approaching it from the southwest, look for the road opposite St. Ann's Catholic Church, a few minutes drive east of Hedley.

● ● ●

Additional Information Sources

Apex Alpine
P.O. Box 1060,
Penticton, B.C. V2A 7N7
Tel: (604) 292-8222

B.C. Parks
Okanagan District,

P.O. Box 399,
Summerland, B.C. V0H 1Z0

Nickel Plate Cross Country
Ski Club
P.O. Box 27,
Penticton, B.C. V2A 6J9.

● ● ●

19

Cathedral Provincial Park

Statistics	For map, see page 93.
Distance:	25 km, Keremeos to Cathedral Base Camp.
	15 km, Base Camp to Cathedral Lakes Lodge.
Travel Time:	Two to three hours, Keremeos to Lodge.
Elevation gain:	1585 metres, Keremeos to Cathedral Lks Lodge.
Condition:	Paved , then gravel. Private access to Lodge.
Season:	Best in dry weather. May be closed in winter.
Topo Maps:	Princeton, B.C. 92H/SE (1:100,000)
Forest Map:	Penticton and Area.
Communities:	Keremeos and Princeton.

Wilderness With Access

British Columbia's mountain roads can put anyone's resources to the test, whether they be mental, physical or vehicular. Steep grades, sharp turns, narrow bridges, muddy ruts and windfalls can take the fun out of heading. Those same conditions can change your family sedan to a creaky, muddy mess—or worse—in a matter of a few kilometres. For some of us, the choice is to buy a four-wheel-drive vehicle, stock it up with spare parts, maps and emergency supplies and then boldly set out in search of back-country roads to explore.

Cathedral Lakes Lodge, in Cathedral Provincial Park, offers a second choice. For a fee, they will take you into the heart of one of B.C.'s finest wilderness areas. The round trip fee applies only if you are camping at the park wilderness campsites. If you are staying at Cathedral Lakes Lodge, transportation is included in the accommodation fee. It is worth noting that the road is restricted to park use permit holders and advance reservations are normally required, so plan ahead.

Cathedral Lakes wilderness, in the Okanagan Range of the Cascade Mountains south of Keremeos, has drawn lovers of nature for nearly a century. Before the road, hikers and horsemen followed difficult trails through narrow mountain valleys and along windswept ridges to reach the heart of what is now Cathedral Provincial Park.

The rough trails didn't deter them from returning to this hidden paradise—a cluster of half a dozen clear cool lakes, at over 2,000 metres (6,500 feet) above sea level, surrounded by picturesque ridges and alpine peaks that reach up to 2,628 metres (8,622 feet). The present road and excellent trail system opened up the Cathedrals to a much broader range of visitors. Seniors and youngsters can also reach the lodge or park campgrounds in the Quiniscoe Lake area where the options are many—and all quite spectacular.

"Trails are well marked so that even a novice hiker can reach these places without any danger," says Ches Lyons, the man who, nearly half a century ago, recommended that the park be created. "Whether it is a pleasant forest walk around the lakes or a climb to spectacular vistas and geological wonders, Cathedral Park has it all in a remarkably convenient area for the novice as well as the professional mountaineer."

Wildlife and wildflowers also make the park worth exploring. Ches Lyons book, *Trees, Shrubs and Flowers to know in British Columbia*, has been the B.C. naturalist's Bible for forty years and his suggestions about the local plant life are worth noting.

"Cathedral Park is in the dry interior where the weather is dependable. Towards the end of July and into the first week in August there is a very fine wildflower display. Meadows and swales are bright with lupine, Indian paintbrush, wood betony and veronica. Shrubby cinquefoil, a plant with flowers that look like buttercups, grows in dense masses on some of the slopes.

"White heather and red heather come into bloom just as the peak of the flowers is passing. On the higher elevations all of the plants are adapted to harsh weather and press close to the ground. Many have small hairy leaves to resist water evaporation. Willow grows only an inch or two high. In the spring it flaunts pussy willows as large as those growing on large shrubs."

According to local historians, Indians who lived along the Similkameen and Ashnola Rivers knew of these high mountain lakes long before the arrival of the fur traders. They came here in summer to trap hoary marmots, from which they made valuable blankets. An International Boundary Survey recorded these magnificent mountains

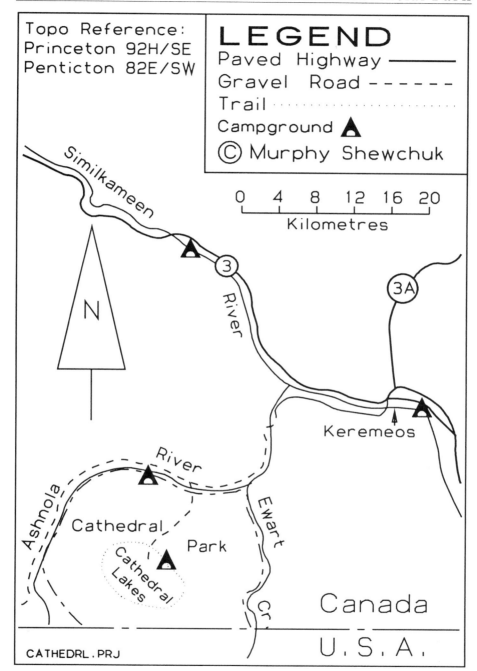

Topo Reference:
Princeton 92H/SE
Penticton 82E/SW

LEGEND
Paved Highway ———
Gravel Road - - - - - -
Trail ·················
Campground ▲
Ⓒ Murphy Shewchuk

0   4   8   12   16   20
Kilometres

Similkameen

3

3A

N

River

Keremeos

River

Ashnola

Cathedral

Ewart

Park

Cathedral Lakes

Cathedral

Cr.

Canada

U.S.A.

CATHEDRL.PRJ

Map 13: Keremeos and Cathedral Park Area.

and sparkling lakes for the first time in 1860. Cathedral Mountain, from which the area gets its name, was named in 1901 by Carl and George Smith because it looked "something like a big church."

Cathedral Lakes Lodge and the provincial park owe their humble beginnings and preservation to two men with foresight and determination. Herb Clark of Keremeos fell in love with the land as a young man of 19. He then went to work in the mines to save money to purchase his dream. In 1934, with about $500 saved, he purchased two parcels of land from the British Columbia government. One parcel was located on Quiniscoe Lake and the other between Glacier and Pyramid Lakes. Next he established a horseback guiding service.

Ches Lyons, then head of British Columbia's three-man Parks Branch, first visited the area about five years after Herb Clark bought his land: "Jim McKeen (Mt. McKeen), a schoolboy friend, swears I was in there in 1939, but I can't remember," writes Ches Lyons in a November, 1991 letter. "I did go in with Joe Harris—Herb's partner—in 1941, had a good look around and recommended it for a provincial park. However, the Forest Service thought there was timberland involved and put a hold on it for many years.

"About 1944, Herb and I rode in, climbed about everything in sight, then made a packhorse trip into the back country. I took 16 mm color film and much of it was used in various films I put together.

"Then Ruth Kirk and I did another trip and made a short film for CBC's Klahanie. The Gehringers were building the lodge at that time."

Herb Clark continued with his efforts to develop a wilderness resort. Before the log cabins were built, he provided the Vancouver Natural History Society with a unique and unforgettable week in this scenic paradise. A story and pictures appeared in the *Vancouver Sun* magazine supplement dated August 25th, 1951. Ernest G. Perrault wrote as follows:

"I have just returned from a camping trip reminiscent of the old days of the West. My companions, like myself, were for the most part greenhorns—members of the Vancouver Natural History Society—accustomed to comfortable strolls through sheltered woods or the shell-littered beaches of this country.

"There were a number of people past fifty, one was seventy; several were school teachers, housewives, telephone operators... And yet here we were climbing uptrail in some of British Columbia's wildest natural surroundings on a warm day in July, determined to pitch camp for seven days above timberline in meadows where carpets of wildflowers grow beside the white ridges of last winter's snow.

Fig. 23: Glacier Lake in Cathedral Park.

"... Picture if you can the sad safari that trudged the fifteen miles into camp that day—rising ever rising—one, two, three thousand feet along trails that switchbacked interminably, clinging like dusty ribbons to the steep mountain slopes. Below us the giant firs fell away and dwindled to small green quills on the valley floors. Above us the lodge pole pine came in more sparsely and mountain juniper sprawled along the ground in twisted gnarls.

"Nine pack horses, each laden with 150 pounds of gear—all our supplies and shelter for the expedition, trudged patiently behind with bells tolling at their necks—overtook us and passed us by. We watched the flicking pendulums of their tails wave us farewell as they passed beyond sight.

"Discouragement had us in a bulldog grip by the time the camp was reached. The sight of white canvas tents in the closing dusk gave us some encouragement. Bowls of hot soup, biscuits and bacon prepared by the advance party gave us a little more.

"But as we lay in our sleeping bags that night seven thousand feet above sea level and listened to the wind, fresh from a race across snowfields, tearing at our tent flaps, we wondered, all of us, how we could possibly endure seven days of this. One thing was certain, we were trapped. An immediate return trip was a physical impossibility.

"Then morning came. First the song of new birds, the horned lark, pipits, whiskey jacks uttering weird mimicry close to the tents. We were amazed to see golden bars of sunlight poking warm fingers through the canvas and when we looked out it was to see a lake as clear as crystal cupped in a shell of granite and snow reaching to the very threshold of the camp. I had brought fishing tackle and watched with satisfaction as silver bodies broke water—one, two, three widening rings that grew until they interlocked.

"The climb had been worth it after all. Day after sunny day we explored the wonders of the Cathedral Lakes. They are named after Cathedral Mountain—an eighty-four hundred foot peak [2,560 metres] carved and eroded into the shape of a ruined abbey. Each lake has a name of its own. We camped on Quiniscoe Lake; half an hour's hike brought us to Lake of the Woods, Pyramid Lake and Glacier Lake, strung like three aquamarines on the same white chain of a mountain stream. Further up still is Lady Slipper and as crystalline as the one Cinderella wore.

"Here was a naturalist's paradise. Two professors from the University of British Columbia, agronomist Dr. Vernon Brink, president of the Natural History Society, and botanist Dr. T. Taylor led parties into the

Fig. 24: Giant Cleft.

meadows, beyond the rocky inclines of scree and lava upthrusts, up into the snow to the very summits of Pyramid and Cathedral Mountains.

"... In following days we fished for cutthroat and Kamloops trout and caught our limits in a few hours. An outcropping of excellent fossils was discovered and we puttered around below old lava formations collecting specimens of sequoia, horsetail and other leaf imprints estimated to be ten million years old. There were campfire sessions when we discussed the finds of the day. And at all times camera shutters recorded the antics of campers as well as the beauties of nature that waited for us around every corner.

"It was a greenhorn expedition. Guide and proprietor Herb Clark must have shaken his head in wonderment at the strange garb and motley manners of this party of City Slickers. But it was a holiday to remember and we proved one point—the beauties of nature are there for the taking—anyone, yes anyone, can have them for the price of a few stiff muscles."

Herb Clark, with partners Tom Fleet and Karl and Helmut Gehringer, formed Cathedral Lakes Resort Ltd. in 1964. Work on
a private road was completed in 1965 and construction was started on
the present buildings.

Cathedral Provincial Park was officially established in 1968,
nearly 30 years after Ches Lyons made his recommendations.
According to Lyons, "Geologically, the park is fascinating and presents
many facets. Except for the highest peaks, glaciers of the last ice age
have rounded the mountain slopes. As the glaciers receded, the ice on
the northern slopes lingered and created large bowls called cirques. This
was done by a long process of water melting and then freezing in the
rock beneath, breaking them apart. The volcanic nature of some of the
mountains is demonstrated in the Devil's Fenceposts which are sym-
metrical columns now twisted and bent but resembling a huge piling of
wood. In Stone City (or Hamburger City) there are most unusual formations of rocks shaped into massive discs. They are considered so
unusual that a geologist did his Master's thesis on them. At the Giant
Cleft you will find a split in the rock face of the mountain caused by
some tremendous forces of the past. Geologists believe the impressive
cleft was caused by the erosion of an intrusion of softer rock. Smokey
the Bear is another impressive rock formation close by. In silhouette, it
appears as a gigantic replica of the forest-fire-fighting ursine complete
with his forest ranger hat. It's a picture you can't duplicate."

Cathedral Provincial Park is indeed a picture you can't duplicate. It
is a unique piece of British Columbia that offers those unable to spend
a day of hard slogging the opportunity to explore this wilderness on the
same footing as those better able to surmount the challenge of getting
there. Once at camp, whether the lodge or the nearby park campgrounds,
the irresistible draw of the Giant's Cleft, alpine wildflowers and tur-
quoise lakes beckons everyone. Go prepared to enjoy Nature at her
finest—and toughest. Don't forget your boots, warm clothing, slicker
and water bottle. Above all, don't forget your film.

•••

Additional Information Sources

Cathedral Lakes Lodge	B.C. Parks
R.R. 1, Cawston, B.C.	P.O. Box 399,
V0X 1C0	Summerland, B.C.
Tel: (604) 499-5848	V0H 1Z0

•••

Fairview Road

Statistics   For map, see page 103.

Distance:	8 km, Keremeos to Cawston.
	24 km, Cawston to Oliver.
Travel Time:	Approximately 1 hour.
Elevation Gain:	700 metres (2,300 feet).
Condition:	Narrow, some rough gravel.
Season:	May be closed in winter.
Topo Maps:	Penticton, B.C. 82 E/SW (1:100,000).
Forest Map:	Penticton and Area.
Communities:	Keremeos, Cawston and Oliver.

A Grist Mill and a Gold Mine

Fairview Road, linking Cawston in the Similkameen Valley and Oliver in the Okanagan Valley, can provide a glimpse of the colorful mining history of the region and a cool alternative to the midsummer heat of the valley. The western end of the road can be approached from several points between Keremeos and Cawston. In the following description, I have chosen to follow Upper Bench Road from Highway 3A because of the special attraction of the historic Keremeos Grist Mill. This route also usually has light traffic, and the scenic contrast of the orchards below the stark mountainside presents some interesting photographic opportunities.

The junction of Highway 3A and Upper Bench Road, one kilometre north of the junction of Highways 3 and 3A makes a good starting point (kilometre 0.0) for a leisurely trip over Orofino Mountain. Upper Bench Road parallels the main valley eastward, cutting a path through the orchards and along the barren cliffs.

Fig. 25: Pumpkin display at Barrington Market in Keremeos.

The Keremeos Grist Mill, less than a kilometre from Highway 3A, is the first stop along the way. Keremeos Creek gurgles through the sheltered vale, providing motive power for the giant wheel in summer and a welcome reason to meander around the site. This grist mill is the only nineteenth-century mill in British Columbia that still has most of its machinery intact. This includes the original flour mill, a Eureka buckwheat screen, grain chute and corn grinding machine as well as a later roller mill.

The original mill was built in 1877 by Barrington Price, who had pre-empted land near Keremeos in 1873. The water-powered mill was operated by John Coulthard after 1885, and served the needs of the Similkameen Valley ranching community for almost 20 years before stiff competition from larger mills, in both quality and price, forced it to close.

In 1974, the mill and adjacent log building were designated an historic site and the slow process of restoration was begun. The Keremeos Grist Mill was officially reopened in 1985, and has since been steadily improved.

Beyond the grist mill, the road passes through the orchards and then along the base of the barren mountain. This country is too dry for timber

Fig. 26: Keremeos Grist Mill on Upper Bench Road.

at the lower elevations, and all that thrives are the desert plants more common to the Cascade Mountain rain-shadow much farther south in Washington and Oregon states.

Orchardists advertise fresh fruit and vegetables in season, and some of the best spring asparagus comes from Keremeos. Local bee keepers also sell orchard blossom honey and beeswax candles. Upper Bench Road continues east until it merges with Highway 3, east of Cawston. However, Lowe Drive, at km 7.7 marks the start of the mountain road to Oliver.

Because of the option to leave Highway 3 at Cawston and avoid the orchard part of the trip, the junction of Lowe Drive and Upper Bench Road has been chosen as kilometre 0.0 of the backroad drive over Orofino Mountain. In the past, a nearby signpost offered a warning to those piloting large recreational vehicles—one that should still be heeded. It read, "Road closed in winter. Not recommended for vehicles other than cars and pickups."

The pavement ends at km 1.2, and as though not to waste any time getting away from the Similkameen Valley, the road quickly begins a northeast climb up Blind Creek. The desert environment, complete with ponderosa pine, sagebrush, prickly-pear cactus and the sunflower blossoms of arrowleaf balsamroot in spring, gives way to gullies lined with stands of cottonwood and aspen.

About the same time as the surroundings get a little damper, the steep grade and tight corners give way to a wider road with an easier grade at km 3.7. The climate continues to change as the road reaches the height-of-land at km 10.0. Now the timber is Interior fir and vine maple bushes hang over the narrow road where it swings near the creek. Watch for cattle—they seem to believe that they have the right-of-way by virtue of being there first.

The road now swings south as it begins its descent into the Okanagan Valley. A side road north to Ripley Lake at km 12.2 and another at km 14.1 offer diversions for the backroad explorer interested in striking out on his own. Ripley, Madden and Burnell (Sawmill) lakes are regularly stocked with rainbow trout. All three lakes have small Forest Service recreation sites complete with cartop boat access.

Mill foundations, waste dumps and open shafts at km 16.9 mark the location of the Fairview gold and silver mines. Gold was first discovered in the area in 1887, writes Karen Witte in a brief

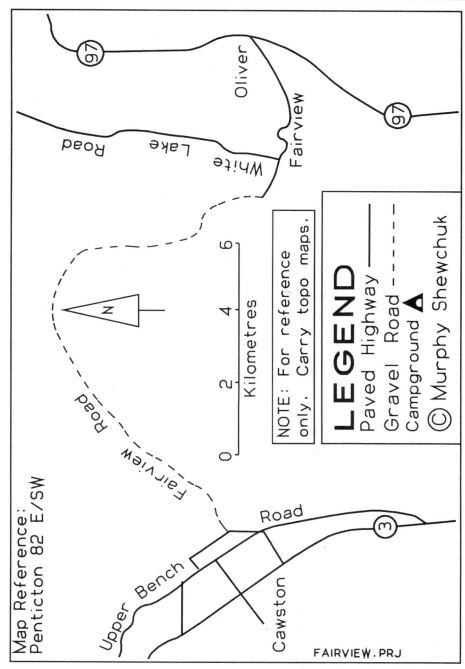

Map 14: Cawston to Oliver via Fairview Road.

Historical Sketch of Fairview. Fred Gwatkins and George Sheenan staked what was later to become the discovery claim of the Stemwinder Mine, the primary instigator of the Fairview Camp. The Stemwinder interests were soon sold to an American and British syndicate and the two-decade first life of the mining camp began when the original Fairview Camp was established near the mine site in 1890.

On August 12, 1892, the first newspaper in Oro, Washington, (now Oroville) published the following account about Fairview: "This camp is in the same gold belt we are, and proves beyond a shadow of a doubt that this is the most extensive mineral belt in the known world."

In 1893, the Golden Gate Hotel (later nicknamed the "Bucket of Blood") opened for business. Within a short time, residential buildings and other commercial developments, including the Miner's Rest, the Fairview, and Moffatt's Saloon, were built on the precarious slopes of the gulch.

But Fairview didn't become a thriving community until the settlement moved down to the mouth of the gulch in 1897, at km 19.3 overlooking present-day Oliver. On July 1, 1899, celebrations marked the opening of the Fairview Hotel (the Big Teepee), the most elegant hostel in the Interior.

It was the fire that destroyed the Big Teepee in 1902 that marked the beginning of the end of Camp Fairview. The gold quartz veins became harder to mine with existing techniques as the mines worked deeper. By World War I, the only real activity was the wrecking bar as salvagers tried to recover the lumber and machinery from the townsite and mills.

The Fairview mines gained a new lease on life two decades later when an executive order issued by U.S. President Roosevelt on January 31, 1934, raised the price of gold from $20.67 to $35.00 per ounce. Gold properties all over the continent saw renewed interest.

Robert Iverson was one of those working the Fairview Amalgamated Mines in 1938. "They had two horses in use pulling a train of five one-ton cars." writes Iverson in the *Okanagan Historical Society 48th Report*. "My job was helping load and unload the train. Between 100 and 150 tons over two shifts were normal... Between 40 and 50 men were employed, including those employed at the mill."

The start of World War II forced the closure of the Fairview and Morning Star properties, but in the half dozen years of renewed operation, they produced 14,000 ounces of gold and 152,000 ounces of silver.

A junction at km 18.2 marks a side road down to south Oliver while the main road keeps left to the junction of Fairview Road and White Lake Road at km 19.3. The gravel road gives way to pavement near the junction and the green orchards of the Okanagan Valley present a contrast to the stark grassland slopes dotted with sagebrush and greasewood in what some claim to be the driest part of Canada.

Fig. 27: Arrowleaf balsamroot near Oliver.

A nearby stop-of-interest sign offers a glimpse of Fairview's past:

FAIRVIEW GOLD

The 1890s held high hopes for the lode gold mines such as Stemwinder, Morning Star and Rattler. By 1902, when the Fairview Hotel or "Big Teepee" burned, the golden years were over. Fairview's population dwindled as miners left for more promising prospects. But some settlers, lured by the natural attractions of the Okanagan Valley, remained to profit from the lasting wealth of its abundant resources.

The "Big Teepee" was the centre of a community that included livery stables, offices, several stores and houses, a school and a government building. Today all that remains of the original buildings is the jail which was moved and reassembled adjacent to the museum in downtown Oliver.

A concrete irrigation flume that passes under the street at km 23 deserves more than a passing glance, for in it is the real gold of the Okanagan Valley. Irrigation in the Okanagan grew out of necessity with techniques that were a carry-over from the water diversion practiced by placer miners. Some of the first water licenses in the Okanagan were recorded in the early 1870s, but serious irrigation didn't begin in the Oliver area of the Okanagan until after World War I.

The *South Okanagan Lands Project* began in 1919, when the B.C. government bought out private holdings amounting to about 9,300 hectares (23,000 acres). A gravity system was constructed to take water from Vaseux Lake. Water was carried across the valley through a siphon that had pipes large enough for men to work inside. The dam and siphon were officially opened by B.C. Premier John Oliver in 1921, but it was not until 1927 that the project, with 100 km of flumes and laterals, was completed and the first irrigation water served the whole area.

Without the foresight and determination of pioneer politicians such as "Honest John" Oliver, the beautiful green orchards and vineyards would still be "just the haunt of jack rabbits and rattlesnakes."

Fairview Road joins Highway 97 at km 23.6 in the heart of Oliver. Across the highway and the Okanagan River, the backroads explorer can continue an eastward trek to Mount Baldy and old Camp McKinney. North of the junction, Highway 97 continues on to Penticton while to the south lies Osoyoos and the U.S. border.

• • •

Additional Information Sources

Okanagan Historical Society 48th Report
Historical Sketch of Fairview by Karen Witte

Oliver and District Chamber of Commerce,
P.O. Box 460,
Oliver, B.C. V0H 1T0

• • •

White Lake Road

Statistics   **For map, see page 108.**

Distance:	32 km, Oliver to Hwy 97 near Kaleden.
Travel Time:	Up to one hour.
Elevation gain:	Minimal.
Condition:	Paved, with some gravel sections.
Season:	Maintained year around.
Topo Map:	Penticton, B.C. 82 E/SW (1:100,000).
Forest Map:	Penticton and Area.
Communities:	Oliver, Okanagan Falls and Penticton.

Listening to the Stars

Clothed in the history of the Okanagan, and of British Columbia, White Lake Road began as an Indian trail. It became the path that David Stuart, of John Jacob Astor's Pacific Fur Company, followed in 1811 for the first white incursion into the valley. In 1821, it became part of the Hudson's Bay Company fur brigade trail between Fort Okanogan on the Columbia River and Fort St. James in northern British Columbia. The last fur brigade, with perhaps two hundred loaded horses, their packers, families and dogs, the beaver-hatted factor and his piper in the lead, camped in the roadside meadows where Hereford cattle graze today.

The establishment of the Canada-U.S.A. boundary in 1846 led to the abandonment of the route as a brigade trail, but as the nineteenth century wore on, it became the route of gold-seekers and cattle drivers heading for the Cariboo. Along it Father Pandosy traveled on his way to establish the church's presence at Okanagan Mission near Kelowna in the late 1850s. As the century closed, this Okanagan backroad echoed to the sounds of creaking wheels and snorting horses as the freight wagons loaded with supplies headed for the gold camps of Camp McKinney and Fairview.

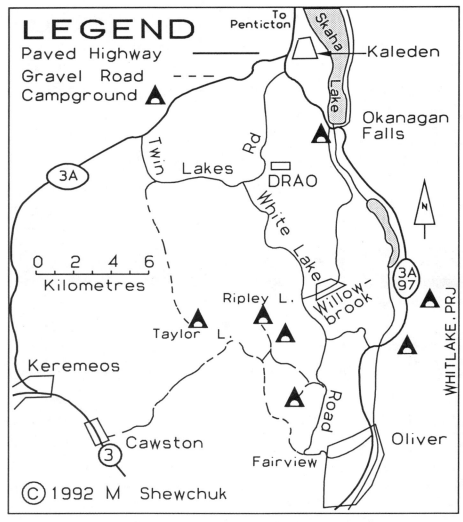

Map 15: Oliver to Kaleden via White Lake Road.

W ith the main traffic light on Highway 97 in downtown Oliver as kilometre 0.0, follow 350th Avenue as it climbs westward. Soon becoming Fairview Road, it leaves the village and orchards to continue up through the sagebrush and greasewood-dotted slopes. Irrigated vineyards cut into the domain of the greasewood, producing one of the Okanagan Valley's finest cash crops.

A stop-of-interest sign near the junction of Fairview Road and White Lake Road, km 4.5, gives a brief glimpse of the long-gone community of Fairview, spawned by the discovery of gold, the Okanagan's oldest cash crop, in a nearby valley. See the *Fairview Road* section (page 99) for more information.

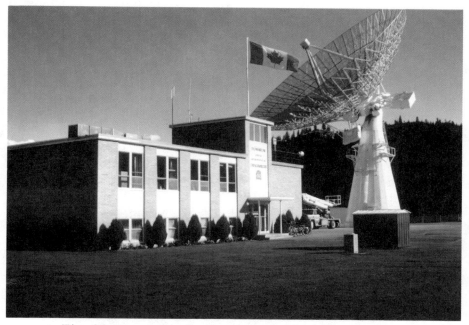

Fig. 28: Dominion Radio Astrophysical Observatory.

White Lake Road follows a dry bench northward, skirting stands of ponderosa pine, sumac bushes, flame red in autumn, and small ranches complete with children on horses. Although paved, this backroad deserves caution to avoid domestic animals and other sight-seeing drivers. The side valley begins to broaden, with homes nestled at the base of the cliffs. Another backroad, near km 12, winds down Park Rill to join Highway 97, north of Oliver.

Green Lake Road, km 16.0, marks the junction to yet another road down to the Okanagan Valley. After passing through the community of Willowbrook, it winds northeast around Mt. Hawthorne, past Mahoney and Green Lakes as it descends to the Okanagan River near Okanagan Falls. Before joining Highway 97 at the bridge, it offers several excellent views of the valley and the highlands to the east.

Beyond the junction, the White Lake Road starts climbing gently at first, then more steeply as the road curves upward between the grassy hills and rock bluffs. Near km 22 the valley opens to a sometimes dry pond (White Lake) and the antenna farm of the Dominion Radio Astrophysical Observatory (D.R.A.O.). The junction with Twin Lakes Road, km 24, presents the option of heading west to Olalla and Keremeos or continuing north to Kaleden. The road to the west (left) passes the Twin Lakes junction (eight kilometres) and joins Highway 3A near Yellow Lake, while the White Lake Road continues north, past the observatory.

The Dominion Radio Astrophysical Observatory can be an extraordinary sight when you first round the corner and catch a glimpse of the group of giant parabolic antennae pointing skyward. The answers to your questions can be answered at the visitor centre which is open daily, with guided tours on Sundays during July and August.

Visitors are asked to park in the lot next to the White Lake Road, at km 25.0, and walk into the observatory site so that vehicle ignition noise will not interfere with the sensitive radio receivers that are part of the operation. These receivers, coupled to the huge parabolic antenna and the pole-top antenna array, are used to study radio emissions from our own sun, moon and planets as well as distant nebulae, supernovae (exploding stars), dark gas clouds and the Milky Way.

In addition to the computer-controlled receivers located at White Lake, computers link the receivers here with those at the Algonquin Radio Observatory near Ottawa, Ontario, simulating an antenna with a 3,074 km baseline, for studies of remote galaxies.

From the radio observatory to Highway 97, the road winds generally downhill with a few steep narrow sections to add to the excitement, particularly after a snowfall or a heavy rain.

White Lake Road emerges from this side valley, at km 32, to join Highway 97 approximately one kilometre south of the junction of Highway 97 and Highway 3A near Kaleden.

•••

Additional Information Sources

Oliver and District Chamber of Commerce,
P.O. Box 460,
Oliver, B.C. V0H 1T0

•••

Mount Baldy Loop

Statistics   For map, see page 115.

Distance:	53 km, Oliver to Highway 3 near Bridesville.
Travel Time:	Two to three hours.
Elevation gain:	1450 metres (4750 feet).
Condition:	Gravel, rough in spots.
Season:	Maintained all year around, muddy in spring.
Topo Maps:	Penticton, B.C. 82E/SW (1:100,000).
Forest Maps:	Boundary District.
Communities:	Oliver, Bridesville and Osoyoos.

From Sand Dunes to Ski Slopes

Backroads explorers are often forced to resort to armchair traveling when the snow closes in on the mountains of British Columbia. This is usually the time to repair fishing equipment, overhaul the vehicle and sort the photographs from the previous trips into the heartland of the province.

There are exceptions, of course, and one is the McKinney Road — Mount Baldy Road loop through the Okanagan Highlands from Oliver to Bridesville. The attractions include B.C.'s Okanagan desert, mountain climbing, rockhounding in old gold diggings and—the reason for year round access—cross-country and alpine skiing at the Mount Baldy Ski Area.

The traffic light at 350th Avenue and Highway 97 in the heart of Oliver serves as kilometre 0.0 and a suitable landmark for the start of this backroad trip into the highlands. Formerly Park Drive, 350th Avenue crosses the Okanagan River near the light. McKinney

Fig. 29: Catching a few rays on Mount Baldy.

Road (362nd Avenue) swings right off 350th Avenue less than half a kilometre from the traffic light on Highway 97.

If you're hell-bent on heading for the hills, take McKinney Road. However, if it's hotter than Hades—as it can be in Oliver—continue straight ahead on 350th Avenue and 79th Street to 370th Avenue (formerly Harrison Way) and then take 370th Avenue and 81st Street to the public beach on Tuc-Ul-Nuit Lake. Also known as Tugulnuit Lake, this spring-fed swimming hole is a welcome break before tackling gravel and dust.

McKinney Road suffers from a minor identity problem with a sign at km 1.1 identifying it as Camp McKinney Road just before it crosses a concrete irrigation flume. At the junction with Sand Point Drive at km 1.9, the "Camp" is dropped.

McKinney Road enters the Inkaneep Indian Reserve and as the paved road swings around a sandy knoll, sagebrush and ponderosa pine begin, leaving the fruit orchards behind. This land is typical of the desert that existed before irrigation turned the bottomland into orchards. It is barren, desolate and HOT. Greasewood, sumac and the occasional clump of bunchgrass cling desperately to the sand dunes that were once under an ancient glacial lake.

Farther up the road, the effects of water are again visible with the desert on one side of the road and on the other side, near Wolfcub Creek, lush green hay fields. Water makes a major difference in this region which is considered to be an extension of the Sonoran Desert of New Mexico.

The road continues to climb southeast into the highlands. Near km 8.0 the desert gives way to another symbol of the dry country—ponderosa pine trees. They are scattered over the hillside, providing resting cattle with pockets of green shade among the clumps bunchgrass.

A small lake near km 16 (14K on the roadside markers) marks the end of the pavement. A close look at a detailed topographic map, or the view from a low-flying aircraft, will reveal countless small man-made lakes and ponds in southern British Columbia's high country. Some of these were originally developed to store water for gold mining operations. But most of them were built to collect the water from winter snows and June rains to supply grazing cattle and to flood-irrigate hay fields when the hot, rainless summer winds sweep up from the American southwest.

The stands of ponderosa pine gradually mix with interior Douglas fir and then needle-shedding larch as the road climbs eastward up the slopes of the Okanagan Highland. In September and October, the larch changes color, adding splashes of yellow to the background of ever-green forest.

A sharp corner near km 22.0 should be treated with respect—the loose gravel and sand traps leave little room for mistakes. Although more than a bit dusty (depending on the season), McKinney Road is still wide and well-built at this point. The height-of-land dividing the Inkaneep Forest and the Kettle Forest near km 30.0 also divides the Highways' districts of the region. A decade ago, the route was virtually impassable beyond the divide, but reconstruction and rerouting of the road has been spurred on by the need for better access to the Mount Baldy Ski Area, the site of the 1985 B.C. Winter Games.

A junction near km 36 marks the last short leg of the trip to Mount Baldy. A short 2.6 kilometre drive up the mountain to the left (north) lies the headquarters of the Mount Baldy alpine ski operation. According to Bill Hatton, a pioneer of the region since 1920, Mount Baldy ski resort had its beginnings in the mid-1960s with the Borderline Ski Club. The Club was formed in 1939 and operated on nearby Anarchist Mountain before moving to the privately-operated Mount Baldy in 1968. In his book, *Bridesville Country*, Hatton writes that a ski tow was set up on the Hedlund ranch on the east side of Anarchist Summit and served local skiers for several years before they embarked on the ambitious project of developing the slopes of Mount Baldy. It took hard work, but the sight of happy skiers on the sunny slopes using the T-Bar tow and a dozen runs is an appropriate monument to their efforts.

In 1985, the club managed the ski races associated with the B.C. Winter Games held at Mount Baldy. This was the peak of the resorts activity, and it then slid downhill when the operators ran into one of the low-snow years that plague all ski resorts. After closing for the 1986-87 season, Mount Baldy has re-opened with a flourish under the careful management of the Borderline Ski Club. The mountain serves skiers from the South Okanagan, Similkameen and West Kettle districts with regular skiers arriving from south of the border in Washington State. The main attractions are its friendly, family-oriented atmosphere and every type of run from beginner to advanced.

The "Halloween Trees," left over from a forest fire that gave the mountain its bald appearance, provide Mount Baldy's trade-mark as well as a challenging and interesting backdrop to glade skiing at the higher elevations of the mountain. And when the mist rolls in, the

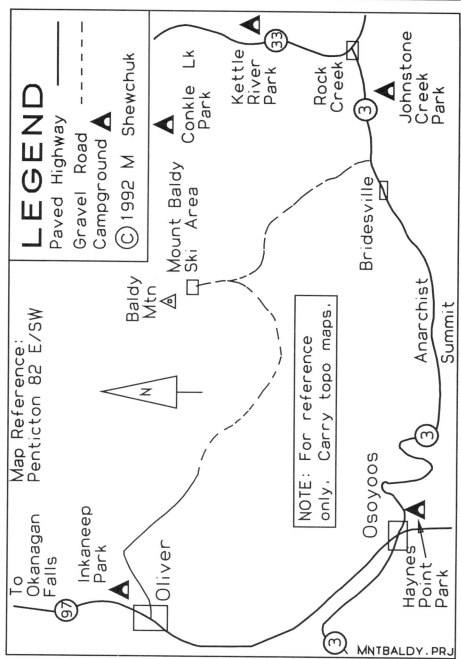

Map 16: Oliver -- Mount Baldy -- Bridesville.

"Halloween Trees" stretch out their gray arms in a way that triggers the imagination and justifies the name.

M t. Baldy Road, to the right of the junction at km 36, was once the only access to the ski resort. It follows the drainage of McKinney and Rice creeks down to join Crowsnest Highway 3 at the Rock Creek Bridge a few kilometres east of Bridesville. The descent toward Highway 3 offers a number of excellent views of the grasslands of Anarchist Mountain and the desert country far to the southwest.

T oday, the Camp McKinney workings, five kilometres from the Mount Baldy junction, are a jumble of abandoned mine shafts, deep crevices, waste heaps, rusting mining equipment and barbed wire fences. It's a dangerous place for stray man or beast, but it wasn't always so...

According to N.L. "Bill" Barlee in *Gold Creeks and Ghost Towns*, Camp McKinney was born in 1887 as one of the earliest lode gold camps in British Columbia. "By 1893," writes Barlee, "the camp was roaring on the strength of excellent assays from claims like the Cariboo, Amelia, Alice, Emma and Okanagan."

The Cariboo-Amelia claim later developed into the premier mine of the camp, even paying dividends to shareholders. By 1901, the population of the camp stood at 250, with hotels, stores, a school and a church among the amenities of the community. Three years later the Cariboo Mine closed and within months Camp McKinney became a ghost town.

Forest fires in 1919 and 1931 destroyed most of the original town and all that remains is a small, decaying log cabin of indeterminate age.

A short note in the B.C. Minister of Mines Report for 1943 states that two groups operating in the old Cariboo-Amelia claim mined 736 tons of ore, yielding 388 oz. of gold, 628 oz. of silver, 7,219 lb. of lead and 5,381 lb. of zinc. A much newer head frame, shaft and service buildings, a short distance east of the decaying cabin, mark more recent efforts to rekindle interest in Camp McKinney.

Beyond the mining camp, the gravel road continues its descent through stands of larch (tamarack) and lodgepole pine before emerging into the grasslands near the McKinney Creek crossing, approximately 51 kilometres from Oliver. A short drive farther and the road climbs up through a sand cut to the benchland high above the junction of McKinney Creek and Rock Creek.

The Oliver—Mount Baldy—Bridesville loop joins Highway 3 at the western approach to the Rock Creek Bridge, one of the tallest bridges on Highway 3. From this point, pavement leads west to Osoyoos via

116

Fig. 30: Mine tipple at Camp McKinney (Sept. 1985).

Anarchist Summit or east to the community of Rock Creek in the Kettle Valley.

A provincial park at Johnstone Creek, a short drive to the east, can serve as an excellent campsite before continuing backroads exploring. If you are interested in camping a little farther off the highway, a gravel road near Johnstone Creek winds northward to Conkle Lake Provincial Park. See *Conkle Lake Loop*, page 119 for details.

• • •

Additional Information Sources

Bridesville Country: A Brief History by Bill Hatton. Printed by Oliver Printing, May 1981.

Gold Creeks and Ghost Towns by N.L. "Bill" Barlee. Published by Hancock House Publishers Ltd., Surrey, B.C. First Printing July, 1970.

Mount Baldy Ski Area,
c/o Borderline Ski Club,
P.O. Box 1528,
Oliver, B.C. V0H 1T0
Tel: (604) 498-2262

Oliver Chamber of Commerce,
P.O. Box 460,
Oliver, B.C. V0H 1T0

B.C. Parks,
West Kootenay District,
RR 3, 4750 Highway 3A,
Nelson, B.C. V1L 5P6

• • •

23

Conkle Lake Loop

Statistics	For map, see page 122.
Distance:	21 km, Highway 33 to Conkle Lake.
	25 km, Conkle Lake to Highway 3.
Travel Time:	Up to one hour on each leg.
Elevation gain:	450 metres.
Condition:	Rough gravel road.
Season:	Best in dry summer weather.
Topo Maps:	Penticton, B.C. 82E/SW (1:100,000).
Communities:	Rock Creek, Beaverdell and Osoyoos.

Backroad to an Upland Getaway

If you're looking for someplace to get away from the crowds, Conkle Lake Provincial Park, located northwest of Rock Creek, does have a charm worth exploring. While the beach at Conkle Lake will never offer serious competition to the broad, sandy beaches at Skaha Lake or Okanagan Lake, it is for this very reason that this small provincial park attracts repeat visitors. Three-kilometre-long Conkle Lake, the dominant feature of the park, lies in a generally north-south direction, with an inviting, sandy beach at the north end. At an elevation of 1,067 metres (3,500 feet), Conkle Lake is slow to warm in the early summer, but when the beaches at Skaha Lake (338 metres or 1,100 feet) are sweltering hot, this upland lake can still be very pleasant.

There are three public routes to 124 hectare (306 acre) Conkle Lake—and all of them are best described as rough and not recommended for motorhomes or vehicles pulling trailers. Judging by the number of motorhomes and trailers at the park when we last camped

119

there, the recommendations mean little to those determined to "get away from it all."

What is probably the most used and least difficult route winds north from Crowsnest Highway 3, 44 kilometres east of Osoyoos and approximately half way between Bridesville and Rock Creek. The signs on Johnstone Creek West Road warn of the impending difficulties, but the first few kilometres are merely steep, twisting and dusty. The transition from open grasslands to lodgepole pine and then to marshland and cedar-lined creek beds is fairly quick. Signs mark the route to Conkle Lake at most of the junctions, particularly where much newer logging roads can create confusion. Much of the road is single lane with intermittent opportunities to pass oncoming traffic and virtually no opportunity to pass any slowpoke in front of you. Caution is essential and a good four-wheel-drive vehicle is a definite asset. A junction approximately 24 kilometres from Highway 3 marks the start of the last short, steep run up to the lake and provincial park. To the left is the park, while straight ahead is the backroad to Highway 33 near Rhone.

T om Evans of Oliver has been fishing Conkle Lake almost every year since 1934. With his help and additional information from Jack Coates, another Oliver resident, I was able to piece together a bit of the puzzle that is the history of Conkle Lake.

According to these gentlemen, two trappers had cabins near the lake well before the 1931 Camp McKinney forest fire destroyed a vast tract of timber north of the Rock Creek bridge. Sullivan and Ripperto were their names, it seems, and they were noted for the private telephone line that they had strung between their cabins. Tom Evans also remembers that Ripperto rawhided high grade gold ore out of a mine he had on one of the nearby mountainsides.

The original road into the lake was a corduroy road, made by laying poles crosswise on a route cut through the upland marshes, put in from the south via Little Fish Lake.

"I've driven it, but it was a real tough drive." says Jack Coates, of Oliver. "It must have been put in way back in the teens or early 20s."

By 1945, the road had disappeared, flooded by beaver dams and overgrown with timber and windfalls. In 1955, Frank Martin bought the land on the north end of the lake and started a fishing camp. He put in a road to the northeast end of the lake from the Johnstone Creek area. Later logging opened up access via the present route into the northwest corner of the lake. As part of his fishing camp, Martin built the two log cabins that are now part of the park maintenance facilities and maintained the camp for three or four years before selling it to Jack Boicy.

120

Fig. 31: Waterfalls in Conkle Lake Park.

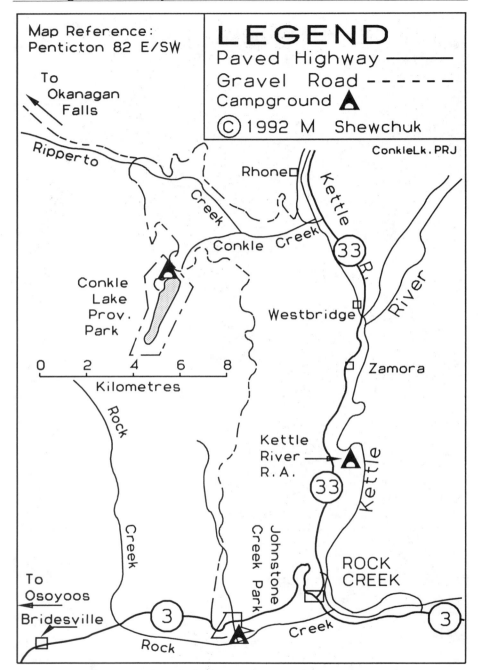

Map 17: Conkle Lake Provincial Park and area.

Boicy operated the camp as Tamarac Lodge for at least a decade with various resident managers in charge. In the early 1970s, Jack was approached by a group that wanted to subdivide the property to build private homes or cottages. Feeling that the property should remain open to the public, he approached south Okanagan sportsmens' clubs and groups such as the Okanagan Similkameen Parks Society for support. With their combined efforts, the provincial government purchased the land in 1972 and began turning it into a park.

Conkle Lake Provincial Park campground is set on benchland in a tamarack (larch) and lodgepole pine forest on the northwest corner of the lake. The vehicle sites are neatly arranged to offer privacy and utility. Services are minimal with no showers, flush toilets or corner store to distract from the back-country camping experience. Make sure your food locker and fuel tank are both full before heading into the park. You may also want to plan your alternatives, should the park be full.

The beach, where tables and a boat launch are located to serve picnickers and fishermen, is only a short walk (or drive) from the campground. The sandy beach is a golden granite type of material with a fairly steep drop-off—good for swimming, but not ideal for non-swimmers or small children.

Fishing, according to the experts and the B.C. Ministry of Environment *Guide to Freshwater Fishing,* is for rainbow trout up to two kilograms. Tom Evans has fished Conkle Lake since 1934. "We used to get a few big trout in those days." says Tom. "We could walk in there and spin cast off the shore or an old raft. We used to get all the fish we wanted."

Hikers will also find the area of interest. An easy trail winds back into the hills to the west of the campground where a beautiful multi-tiered waterfall is hidden. It's about a half hour walk, if you're not in any rush, and the best time to get sunlight on the falls is in mid-morning. A hiking trail is also being developed around the lake although it is only completed along the east shore.

With the park headquarters as kilometre 0.0, the backroad to the north offers two options. Keep left at the junction at km 1.2 and follow the narrow road northwest through an even narrower canyon between km 4.0 and 5.0. A junction at km 5.5, marked R200 or Ripperto Forest Service Road, is the start of a 52 kilometre shortcut to Okanagan Falls. If you continue straight ahead, you should have a relatively uneventful trip down to the West Kettle River and Highway 33 at Rhone, about 15 kilometres to the northeast.

123

If the irresistible lure of the backcountry beckons, as it often does to us, you can swing west up Ripperto Creek and explore the maze of logging roads in the upland plateau. Although I certainly wouldn't guarantee that they are still passable, we traveled this route in the summer of 1991 with little difficulty.

With the R200 signpost as kilometre 0.0, we climbed steadily to the divide at km 6.3, keeping left at km 1.8 and right at a log landing at km 3.7. The divide, at about 1,750 metres (5,740 feet), separates Ripperto Creek from the Kelly River drainage. With compasses at the ready, we switch-backed down to the Kelly River. After a leisurely lunch at an excellent Forest Service recreation site, we continued west over the marshy divide into the headwaters of Vaseux Creek.

The logging roads got progressively better as we drove westward on Road 200 to a junction near kilometre 36.0, (12K on the roadside markers). Here we decided to take the steep winding road down the edge of Shuttleworth Canyon, and around the Weyerhaeuser mill yard to Okanagan Falls and Highway 97.

Ⅰf you have plenty of time, you can detour into Solco Lake "named after the South Okanagan Land Company," says Jack Coates. Or you can take the road to the right at the junction with the 12K marker and continue north on the upland logging roads to Highway 33 near the Big White Ski Resort junction.(See *West Kettle Route*, page 33, for details.)

If you're looking for a backcountry getaway and a place to beat the summer heat—consider Conkle Lake Provincial Park.

●●●

Additional Information Sources:

B.C. Parks
Okanagan District,
P.O. Box 399,
Summerland, B.C. V0H 1Z0

B.C. Parks
West Kootenay District,
RR 3, 4750 Highway 3A,
Nelson, B.C. V1L 5P6

●●●

Haynes Point Park

Statistics   **For map, see page 126.**

Distance:	3 km, junction of Hwy 3 & 97 to 32 Ave.
	1.5 km, east from Hwy 97 on 32 Ave.
Condition:	Paved access road. May be difficult to find.
Season:	Year around.
Topo Maps:	Penticton, B.C. 82 E/SW (1:100,000).
Communities:	Osoyoos and Oroville.

A Sandspit in Osoyoos Lake

Haynes Point Provincial Park is located at the extreme southern end of the Canadian portion of the Okanagan Valley, approximately 2.5 kilometres southwest of the town of Osoyoos. (This valley becomes the Okanogan on the south side of the international border.)

Haynes Point Provincial Park was established in 1962 on 15 hectares (37 acres) of unique and interesting parkland—a narrow sandspit in Osoyoos Lake and an adjacent marsh.

The park was named after Judge John Carmichael Haynes, a noted frontier jurist who brought law and order to the gold fields of Wildhorse Creek, near the present city of Cranbrook. The history of the Haynes family in the Okanagan region goes back to the Rock Creek gold rush where, in 1860, John Carmichael Haynes was sent to assist the Gold Commissioner. Haynes was soon appointed Gold Commissioner as well as Customs Collector. His career didn't stop there, for his subsequent appointments included Member of the Legislative Council of B.C. and County Court Judge. Haynes acquired land at Osoyoos (then called Sooyoos) in 1866, and built a large home on the northeast side of the lake before his sudden death in 1888.

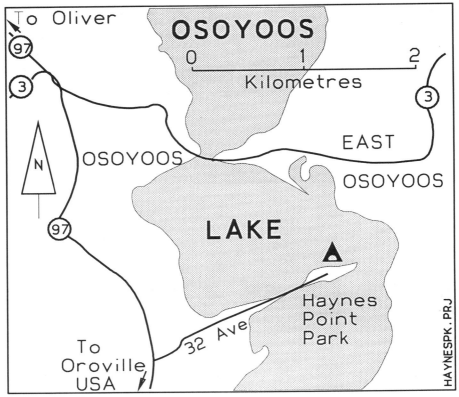

Map 18: Osoyoos and Haynes Point Park.

The region around Haynes Point Provincial Park is also steeped in history. North of the park, Highway 3 crosses a sandspit that was used by fur traders, explorers, miners, and resident Indian populations as a land bridge in their travels up and down the valley. The old Hudson's Bay Company Fur Brigade Trail passed through this very spot, nearly two centuries ago.

Haynes Point Provincial Park is situated in an area which can boast of having Canada's only true desert. It receives less than 35 cm of rainfall per year, and enjoys long, sunny days and cool nights. The entire region is dominated by sagebrush, greasewood, prickly pear cactus and ponderosa pine. As one might expect, much of the wildlife is exotic and some species are found nowhere else in Canada. The short-horned lizard and the desert night snake, for instance, have only been reported a few times this century. These two reptiles share their desert home with many other unusual creatures, such as the secretive spadefoot toad and the burrowing owl.

The bird life is exceptional and varied, especially in the marsh area of the park. A visitor might see canyon wrens, white-throated swifts, or red-winged blackbirds, and for those few with eyes keen enough to spot them, those imperceptible specks circling so high above the valley floor could just be turkey vultures.

Haynes Point Provincial Park contains 41 campsites, each only a few metres from the beach. Osoyoos Lake is reputed to be the warmest lake in Canada, and visitors to the park are likely to have excellent weather for swimming, boating, picnicking, and sun-tanning. The park has a day-use area with picnic tables, a boat ramp, flush toilets, a change-house, horseshoe pits, and a security patrol. Interpretive programs are presented from late June through the Labour Day weekend. Additional activities include nature study and fishing—there are rainbow trout and bass in the lake.

Haynes Point Provincial Park has long been a popular destination for visitors to the Okanagan. As a result the park has instituted a numbering system which provides campsites on a first come, first served basis during the busy season.

The desert isn't all sagebrush and cactus. Some of the Okanagan's finest orchards, vineyards and gardens have been established where water can be pumped for irrigation. The Oliver-Osoyoos area has what is probably the highest number of fruitstands per kilometre of any area in Canada. From May to November, fresh fruit and vegetables are readily available direct from the producer almost anywhere along Highway 3 or Highway 97.

•••

Additional Information Sources

B.C. Parks
Okanagan District,
P.O. Box 399,
Summerland, B.C. V0H 1Z0

Osoyoos Chamber of Commerce
P.O. Box 227,
Osoyoos, B.C. V0H 1V0
Tel: (604) 495-7142

•••

127

Fig. 32: Ferreira's Fruit Market in East Osoyoos.

25

The Okanagan Desert

Statistics	For map, see page 132.
Distance:	12.6 km, Oliver south to Road 22.
	8.0 km, Osoyoos north to Road 22.
Travel Time:	Approximately 15 minutes.
Condition:	Paved highway.
Season:	Year around.
Topo Maps:	Penticton, B.C. 82 E/SW (1:100,000).
Forest Maps:	Penticton and Area.
Communities:	Oliver and Osoyoos.

Osoyoos Oxbows & Haynes Reserve

The environments of the dry benchlands and the Okanagan River floodplain of the South Okanagan Valley are unique to British Columbia and Canada. These environments, in their natural state, support abundant and varied plant and animal life equally unique and valuable to man. The marshlands of the Okanagan River floodplain serve as one of the major migration resting areas and one of the few wintering areas for waterfowl in the interior of British Columbia.

According to a B.C. Ministry of Environment report: "Up to one million ducks, one hundred thousand Canada Geese and thousands of other aquatic birds migrate annually through the Okanagan Valley... These birds attract, in turn, a variety of the often more spectacular raptorial birds such as hawks, falcons, eagles, vultures and owls."

Many other birds also use this area to nest and rear their young. And many species of dryland plants and animals, some of which are believed to be rare or endangered, are found here and not elsewhere in B.C. or Canada.

129

Man, unfortunately, has altered the natural state of the Okanagan environment to the detriment of the original inhabitants. The floodplain became the basis for extensive fruit farming and other agricultural pursuits. Then, when Nature persisted in its normal cycles, the Okanagan River was channeled to reduce flooding of the surrounding farmland. When most of the bottomland was taken up, agriculture, recreation and housing moved up to the benches, displacing the plants and animals that had adapted to the hot, dry environment.

Efforts are, however, under way to preserve segments of the desert environment that have not been totally altered. The Haynes Lease Ecological Reserve, butting on the northeast corner of Osoyoos Lake, is one example of several steps being taken in the area. The reserve contains three distinct land forms; the Okanagan River floodplain, gently sloping terraces above the floodplain, and the steep, southwestern slopes of Inkaneep (Throne) Mountain. The southwest facing slopes, well-drained soils and the rain shadow effect of the Cascade Mountains combine to make this area the most arid in Canada.

The three definable physical zones result in 13 identifiable plant communities varying from cattail wetlands to sumac thickets on the mountain face. In between grow scattered ponderosa pine, fields of antelope brush, sage and rabbitbush, and prickly-pear cactus, arrowleaf balsamroot and bluebunch wheatgrass.

The list of species of birds, mammals and insects that survive (and even thrive) in this harsh environment is too long to present here, but a few are worth mentioning. Rare birds include the canyon wren, sage thrasher and burrowing owl. Rattlesnakes occur in rocky sites and, according to the Ecological Reserves Program report, "the western skink and short-horned lizard are expected to be present." The warm, weedy wetlands are home to largemouth and smallmouth bass and black crappies—fish not usually associated with British Columbia.

Ducks Unlimited is involved with a program to re-water the Okanagan River oxbows that were left dry when the river was channeled in 1958. Working in conjunction with the Ministry of Environment and other interested groups, DU built a weir and control valve that feeds water into 48 hectares (118 acres) of former marshland in what has become known as the Osoyoos Oxbows.

Access to the area is easy. Road 22 leaves Highway 97 on the west side of the Okanagan Valley approximately 12.6 kilometres south of downtown Oliver or eight kilometres north of the junction of Highway 97 and 3 in Osoyoos. It crosses the valley floor and then a bridge over the flood control channel at km 1.1. Although there are gates on the

Fig. 33: Historic Haynes Ranch building at Road 22.

channel dikes, the east dike was open to traffic in both the north and south direction in the spring of 1992. The dike road to the south ends at Osoyoos Lake, 1.8 kilometres from the bridge, with several opportunities to watch waterfowl or osprey, launch a cartop boat or canoe in the flooded oxbows, or fish the channel.

Road 22 runs into Black Sage Road at km 1.6 near the historic, but dilapidated Haynes Ranch House. This building apparently dates back to the late 1800s, but time and vandals have taken their toll. Black Sage Road continues south for two kilometres to the Inkaneep Indian Reserve, and walk-through gates to the lower and upper sections of the ecological reserve. Vehicles aren't permitted and hikers should stay on the old roads to minimize damage to the fragile desert environment.

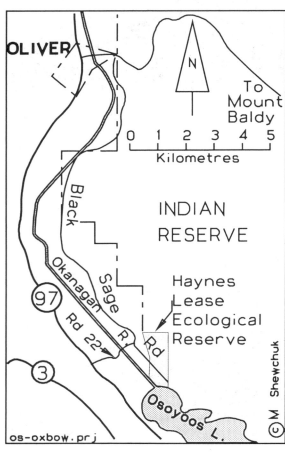

A signed road to the right, a few hundred metres to the north of the Haynes Ranch House on Black Sage Road, leads steeply up to a parking area and access to the upper section of the ecological reserve. Here you can walk south along an old road that takes you into the heart of the upper bench. Watch for cactus, grouse and pheasants underfoot and burrowing owls on nearby fence posts.

Black Sage Road continues north to Oliver along the east side of the valley, joining Camp McKinney Road at km 14.4 and rejoining Highway 97 at km 15.5. (See the *Mount Baldy Loop* section on page 111 for details on access from Oliver.)

Map 19: Oliver to Osoyoos Lake.

•••

26

North Okanagan: An Overview

Vernon and Area

The North Okanagan forms a transition zone between the hot, dry southern reaches of the Okanagan Valley and the wetter, more moderate Shuswap region. The physical division between the two drainage basins, however, is barely perceptible. If it were not for a geographical marker north of Armstrong, most travelers would not notice the change.

The North Okanagan region offers many unique recreational opportunities. Silver Star Ski Resort ranks among the best in the province and western North America. The skiing and snowmobiling trails here become hiking, biking and horse riding trails in mid-summer, presenting an opportunity to explore sub-alpine forests and alpine meadows not often found elsewhere in the world. South of Vernon, less than an hour from Silver Star, the semi-desert rocky ridges and emerald green bays of Kalamalka Lake Provincial Park present a sharp contrast to the forested alpine. With sheltered, sandy beaches and 10 kilometres of trails through the grasslands, it is an attractive recreation destination.

And somewhere between the two climatic extremes lies several other parks. Ellison Provincial Park, southwest of Vernon on Okanagan Lake, also has rocky bluffs, sheltered bays and sandy beaches, but it has a few more trees to keep it a touch cooler in mid-summer. Mabel Lake Provincial Park, higher and farther into the Monashee Mountains, north of Lumby, has sandy beaches and clear water in the heart of the forest.

When you've had your fill of strenuous activity, Historic O'Keefe Ranch, northwest of Vernon, is open all year around for a glimpse of the area's colorful past. The museum in Vernon, the Armstrong Fair and a host of other diversions will also keep you enjoyably occupied.

While researching and writing this book, it quickly became apparent that the region could easily fill a book of its own, thus what I offer here is only a brief glimpse at what lies off the beaten track. May it whet your appetite enough to keep you exploring until that book is written.

May we meet along the way.

•••

Fig. 34: Okanagan Lake and headlands at Ellison Park.

Ellison Provincial Park

Statistics	For maps, see pages 136 & 149.
Distance:	16 km, from the junction of Hwy 97 and 6.
Travel Time:	One half hour.
Elevation Gain:	Minimal.
Condition:	Paved throughout.
Season:	Year around.
Topo Maps:	Vernon, B.C. 82 L/SW (1:100,000).
Forest Maps:	Vernon and Area.
Communities:	Vernon and Okanagan Landing.

Rocky Headlands and Sheltered Coves

Located just 16 kilometres from downtown Vernon, on the north-eastern shore of Okanagan Lake, 200 hectare (500 acre) Ellison Provincial Park is a land of rocky, forested headlands and sheltered, sandy bays. The diverse terrain, combined with the North Okanagan's relatively dry climate (less than 40 cm of precipitation per year) and abundant sunshine, makes it a favorite for a wide range of recreational activities.

To get there, take 25th Avenue west from the junction of Highway 97 and Highway 6 on the south side of downtown Vernon. Follow 25th Avenue as it becomes Okanagan Landing Road, and continue south along the east shore of Okanagan Lake to the end of the road at the park.

Fifty-four private, yet spacious campsites, suitable for most types of camping units, are tucked into an attractive natural forest setting with toilets and firewood nearby. A children's playground is located in the large grassed playing field near the amphitheatre. For additional security there is a resident park contractor. A campground host is also on site from May through September to answer questions.

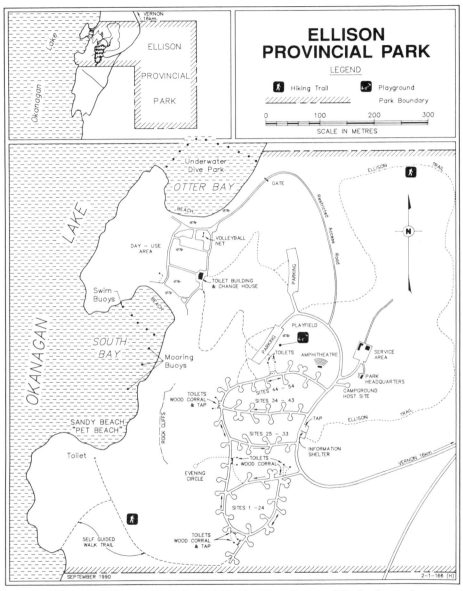

Map 20: Ellison Provincial Park (Courtesy of B.C. Parks).

E asy walking trails provide access to the lakeshore where rocky headlands separate two beautiful bays, with coarse sandy beaches. Here, scattered under the shade of the forest canopy, are more than 50 picnic tables with fire pits. Drinking water and firewood are nearby and the large change house includes flush toilets and showers. The various trails across the rocky headlands provide some boulder-climbing excitement for young explorers and an opportunity to bird watch or photograph the scenery and wildflowers.

The gradually sloping bottom and the warm water make the three main beaches very popular during the summer months. For safety reasons, swim buoys at South Beach closely follow the edge of an underwater shelf. Watch for steep drop-offs outside the buoys and anywhere along the rocky cliffs edges. Please remember that there are no lifeguards on duty. Don't swim alone and watch your children whenever they are near or in the water.

S cuba diving/snorkeling buoys in Otter Bay mark the boundaries of western Canada's first freshwater dive park, sponsored by the Vernon Scuba Club and B.C. Parks. Sunken artifacts add to the variety of fascinating plant and animal life that thrive in the bay's warm waters.

Abundant fish life—including carp, burbot, kokanee and trout—is attracted to the rocky outcroppings and vegetation along the lake front. The best fishing is in the deeper waters offshore anywhere along the north arm of Okanagan Lake. A B.C. angling license is required.

While there isn't any boat launch at the park (the closest is six kilometres to the north), water skiing, cruising, and fishing are popular park activities. Mooring buoys offshore in South Bay and Otter Bay are part of a marine park system sponsored by the Okanagan's yacht clubs. Houseboats can pull ashore at Sandy Beach. The standard park camping fee is charged for overnight use by boaters. If staying in the campground you can leave your boat pulled up on the beach, but please remove all life jackets and other equipment for safe keeping.

T rail guides are available at the park for over six kilometres of walking trails that provide access to many of the park's natural features and scenic viewpoints. A $1\frac{1}{2}$ hour return walk on the nature trail will take you up and down the undulating benches typical of this portion of the Thompson Plateau. Most of the park is dominated by ponderosa pine and Douglas fir stands with grassy open areas and rocky outcroppings along the headlands. Porcupine and Columbian ground squirrels are commonly seen near the nature trail.

A park interpreter is in attendance from mid-June through Labour Day to provide a variety of entertaining and informative programs on the area's human and natural heritage. Highlights during the season are the children's programs and special visits from the McMillan Planetarium. Because of the distance from the city lights, Ellison's clear night sky provides some of the best star viewing in the Okanagan.

Ellison Provincial Park can also be an excellent base from which to explore the North Okanagan. The region's climate has supported its position as a prime fruit growing and ranching area since the mid 1800s. Cycling the rolling hills past orchards, farms and ranches can be an excellent family activity. Historic O'Keefe Ranch, northwest of Vernon, is open all year and it is well worth exploring. (See the *Westside Road* section, page 147, for more information.)

Kalamalka Lake Provincial Park, just east of Vernon, (see page 140) has broad, sandy beaches and 10 kilometres of trails through the grasslands. Mabel Lake Provincial Park, 23 kilometres north of Lumby, (see page 153) has beautiful sandy beaches, open grassy playing fields and great fishing. The 81 unit Mabel Lake campground is not quite as busy mid-week during July and August.

Echo Lake Provincial Park, off Highway 6, 47 kilometres east of Vernon, has picnicking and fishing with boat launch facilities, a store and fishing equipment rentals. Echo Lake Resort in Echo Lake Provincial Park has housekeeping cabins and a campground. Reservations are preferred.

Silver Star Park, 22 kilometres northeast of Vernon, has chairlift operations for summer mountain biking and hiking alpine meadows, with alpine and Nordic skiing in winter. (See the *Silver Star Park* section on page 143 for details.)

• • •

Additional Information Sources:

B.C. Parks
Okanagan District,
P.O. Box 399,
Summerland, B.C. V0H 1Z0

Vernon Tourism,
6326 Highway 97 North,
Vernon, B.C. V1T 6M4
Tel: (604) 542-1415

• • •

Kalamalka Lake Park

Statistics	For maps, see pages 141 & 149.
Distance:	7.6 km, Hwy 97 in Coldstream to parking lot.
Travel Time:	Less than ten minutes, on paved streets.
Season:	Year around.
Topo Maps:	Vernon, B.C. 82 E/SW (1:100,000).
Communities:	Vernon and Coldstream.

Rock Bluffs, Rattlesnakes and Beaches

Fig. 35: Kalamalka Lake, from 10 km south of Vernon.

L ocated on the northeast side of beautiful Kalamalka Lake, Kalamalka Lake Provincial Park encompasses an 890 hectare (2,200 acre) remnant of the natural grasslands that once stretched from Vernon to Osoyoos. Access is easy. If you are traveling from the south on Highway 97, you can turn right on College Way in Coldstream and follow it and then Kickwillie Loop down to Kalamalka Lake. Swing left and follow Westkal Road to Kalamalka Road, keep right past the public beach to Kidston Road (3.8 kilometres from Hwy 97). Turn right on Kidston Road and follow it another 3.8 kilometres to the parking lot. Access from Highway 6 is via Kalamalka Road and Kidston Road.

Kalamalka Lake Provincial Park has all-season appeal. Easy walking and horse riding trails wind through the grassland slopes and along forest ridges. Many scenic viewpoints overlook a shoreline indented with bays and tiny coves. The spring wildflowers are truly spectacular. In summer, the beaches attract boaters and swimmers wanting relative seclusion. The golden hues of autumn have their own appeal. In winter, cross-country skiers enjoy the park's wild beauty and rolling hills.

A s shown on maps posted at the parking lot and trail heads, B.C. Parks has established three distinct colour-coded management zones: These colour-coded zones indicate the facilities provided and the restrictions imposed to reflect the special needs of each area. Red (Jade and Juniper Bays, Cosens Bay Beaches), Yellow (Turtle's Head Point) and Green (Rattlesnake Hill, Bear Valley, Cosens Valley, grasslands) zones have been established to ensure a balance between recreational requirements and the need to protect the park's unique environment.

The range of park activities at Kalamalka Lake Park is unusually wide. Some of the old roads and hiking trails are being upgraded to provide easy walking to the main ecological features and view points. Horse riding is permitted in portions of the park and access to routes through the grasslands and over Rattlesnake Hill are provided at the Red, Watertower, Hydro and Cosens Bay gates. Horses are permitted in the Cosens Bay Beach area, but only from October 31 to March 31.

Bicycle riding is allowed on routes in the grasslands and Rattlesnake Hill. However, it is worth noting that these routes are shared with hikers and horse riders. Juniper Bay has a picnic site just above the beach with tables and grassy play area. A display explaining the park's natural history is located nearby. Swim buoys mark off swimming areas in Jade, Juniper and Cosens Bays. Boaters are encouraged to use Cosens Beach and Jade Beach as well as the many tiny coves between Rattlesnake Point and Cosens Bay. Kekuli Bay Provincial Park, across Kalamalka Lake, has boat-launching facilities.

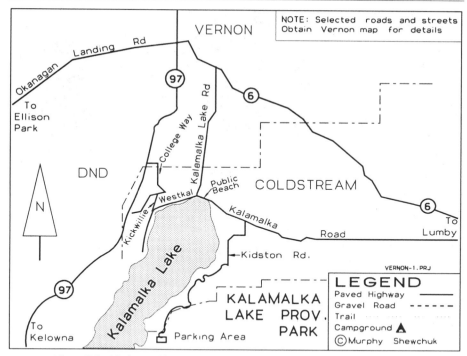

Map 21: Kalamalka Lake Provincial Park access routes.

Kalamalka Lake Park and the surrounding area has a diversity of wildlife although none is particularly abundant. You may see coyote, deer, or black bear but are more likely to observe Columbian groundsquirrels and yellow-bellied marmots. Pacific rattlesnakes, shy creatures that only wish to be left alone, are an important part of this fascinating ecosystem. For botanists, there are four distinct plant associations—arid grasslands, woodland, forest and wet areas—with over 432 species of vascular plant so far identified in the park (10 of these are rare in B.C.).

Please be aware that this is a natural environment protecting one of the few remaining habitats for Pacific rattlesnakes. Practice safe hiking procedures when in rattlesnake country—stay on the trails and watch where you are putting your hands, feet and seat. These animals usually strike only when threatened with no chance to escape. If a bite does occur, try to stay calm and seek medical aid at the Vernon Hospital.

There is another reason to be aware of where you sit. This area was used as a military target range during World War II and unexploded bombs are still working their way to the surface.

Fig. 36: A wary rattlesnake watches a wary photographer.

O f special note to drivers is the fact that Cosens Bay Road is open only to authorized vehicle traffic. Properly licensed motorcycles, trail bikes and mini bikes operated by licensed drivers are permitted in the parking areas, but nowhere else in the park. From a safety perspective, please keep close watch on children: there are no lifeguards in attendance. Deep drop-offs exist outside the buoyed swim areas and along the lakeshore. Cliff jumping can be extremely hazardous because of projecting rock shelves and debris just below the lake surface. Other regulations concerning pets, parking and noise are posted in the park.

• • •

Additional Information Sources:

B.C. Parks
P.O. Box 399,
Summerland, B.C. V0H 1Z0

Vernon Tourism,
6326 Highway 97 North,
Vernon, B.C. V1T 6M4

• • •

Silver Star Park and Village

Statistics

Distance:	22 km, from Hwy 97 in Vernon.
Travel Time:	One half hour.
Condition:	Paved throughout.
Season:	Year around.
Topo Maps:	Vernon, B.C. 82 L/SW (1:100,000).
Communities:	Vernon.

Winter Skiing and Summer Cycling

Fig. 37: Silver Star Village at night.

There are a few who think that mountains have no personalities— that they are mere piles of rock held together by the moss and trees that cover their slopes. These non-believers have obviously never skied the mountains of British Columbia's Okanagan.

Take Silver Star, for example. This peak has a warm, western personality garnered, in part, from the resort staff and the friendly residents of nearby Vernon. First impressions are lasting impressions. And should you arrive in the evening, the first impression at the start of your Silver Star ski vacation is of an 1890s Old Canadian West village.

Silver Star comes by its Old West theme quite honestly. The mountain, originally named Aberdeen Mountain, is believed to have received its present name from the star-like appearance of the peak on a moon-lit winter night and the silver deposits that were discovered near the 1915 metre (6,280 foot) summit in the 1890s. Silver Star was a mining hotspot in 1896 when a quartz vein containing silver, lead and gold was discovered. A forestry lookout was built near the top in 1914 and skiing began in the early 1920s. An access road was built into the area in 1939, setting off the chain of events that led to today's modern development.

Today. the scene on your evening arrival from Vernon is one of well-lit ski slopes, a cozy hotel complex and the mellow lighting of the pedestrian square. Everything is true ski-to-your-door at Silver Star. Night skiing on the lower slopes and a lighted five-kilometre cross-country loop trail are only a few steps from any of the hotels. Daylight broadens the picture. The hotels look bigger—big enough to accommodate more than 650 people. The mountain looks bigger—in fact, with the 1991 opening of the Putnam Creek addition, it's twice as big as it was a few years ago. And the service is even friendlier.

Silver Star offers a blend of skiing under near-perfect conditions. Fine slope grooming often means an earlier start and a longer spring skiing season than other ski resorts. The original Vance Creek area of Silver Star Mountain offered plenty of variety. But the recent opening of the adjacent Putnam Creek development has doubled the skiing terrain to 260 hectares (700 acres), adding considerable intermediate and expert terrain. The addition also makes Silver Star the second largest ski area in British Columbia. For those interested in specs, the mountain now has a vertical drop of 760 metres (2,500 feet) and an average snowpack of 250 centimetres (100 inches). It also had, at last count, over 60 runs served by three quad chairlifts, two double chairs, two T-bars and one handle tow.

Fig. 38: A grouse hen in a sub-alpine meadow.

If you brought your skinny skis, you will be particularly pleased with the range of cross-country ski trails on Silver Star Mountain. A low-cost lift ride takes you to the top of the Summit Chair and the beginning of a well-groomed 15 kilometre loop that brings you back to the hotel complex—with plenty of diversions. The diversions include some 50 kilometres (30 miles) of trails that are part of the Sovereign Lake network in Silver Star Provincial Park and 20 kilometres (12 miles) of groomed trails adjacent to the ski village.

The Sovereign Lake ski trails are operated for B.C. Parks by the North Okanagan Cross Country Ski Club. The club assists with the construction and planning of the ski trails, parking lots and warm-up shelters under a park use permit. A reasonable fee is charged for trail usage to help offset maintenance costs. The Vernon Snowmobile Club has also been involved with trails in the park.

S ilver Star doesn't shut down in summer. From late June until Labour Day, you can join the Silver Star Mile High Descent Tour that takes you from the summit, through alpine meadows, lush forests, grasslands and orchards to the city of Vernon. You and your mountain bike will ride the chairlift to the top and be guided back down via the ski trails and road to a waiting bus which will then take you back up to the ski village. Rental bikes are available. If you find guided tours too restrictive, you can take your time and your camera and explore the mountain trails on foot, bicycle or horseback.

To get to Silver Star, turn east off Highway 97 on 48th Avenue (Silver Star Road) in north Vernon and follow the signs for 22 kilometres to the ski village. Good snow tires are necessary in winter.

• • •

Additional Information Sources:

North Okanagan Cross-Country Ski Club,
P.O. Box 1543,
Vernon, B.C. V1T 8C2

Silver Star Mountain Resort,
P.O. Box 2,
Silver Star Mountain, B.C.
V0E 1G0
Tel: (604) 542-0224

Vernon Tourism,
P.O. Box 520,
6326 Highway 97 North,
Vernon, B.C. V1T 6M4
Tel: (604) 542-1415

B.C. Parks, Okanagan District,
P.O. Box 399,
Summerland, B.C. V0H 1Z0
Tel: (604) 494-0321

• • •

Westside Road

Statistics

For map, see page 149.

Distance:	68 km, Hwy 97 at O'Keefe to 97 at Westbank.
Travel Time:	One hour.
Condition:	Paved, with narrow, winding sections.
Season:	Year around. May be slippery in winter.
Topo Maps:	Vernon, B.C. 82 L/SW (1:100,000).
	Kelowna, B.C. 82 E/NW (1:100,000).
Forest Maps:	Penticton and area.
Communities:	Vernon, Kelowna and Westbank.

Spallumcheen to Westbank

If you're looking for a scenic drive that won't rattle the fenders off the old auto or bring back your migraines with billowing clouds of dust, you might want to take a close look at Westside Road. It has plenty of reasons to recommend it—and few reasons to consider an alternate route. If you've got lots of time, the pluses, such as the historic O'Keefe Ranch, Fintry, Okanagan Lake Resort, Bear Creek Park and numerous lakeside viewpoints, are well worth taking a little extra time. But, if you are in a hurry, consider staying on Highway 97. Nobody hurries on Westside Road and lives to tell about it.

Access can be either from Westbank, southwest of Kelowna, or Spallumcheen, northwest of Vernon. The southern end of Westside Road has been mentioned several times in this book, particularly in connection with Bear Creek Provincial Park and Bear Forest Service Road. Because a larger portion of this byway appears to lie in the North Okanagan, I have chosen to describe it in a north-south sequence, beginning at it's junction with Highway 97 near the O'Keefe Ranch.

147

Fig. 39: Steel-wheel farm tractor at O'Keefe Ranch.

O'Keefe Ranch had its beginning in 1867 when Cornelius O'Keefe and Thomas Greenhow drove a herd of cattle from Oregon to the north end of Okanagan Lake. A year later, O'Keefe homesteaded 65 hectares (160 acres) nearby, and within 40 years his cattle were grazing over 6,000 hectares (15,000 acres) of the North Okanagan's prime grasslands. O'Keefe gradually built up one of the largest cattle empires in the Okanagan, establishing his own community to serve the ranch and its employees. It had a store, post office, blacksmith shop and church—and much of the original equipment and buildings has been preserved in the form of a living ranch museum that is open to the public. To complement the original ranch buildings, the site has a restaurant and gift shop plus other seasonal attractions. For a small entry fee, you can explore the old buildings, many of which contain their original furnishings. In the summer months, you can also ride around the ranch aboard a horse drawn hay wagon.

St. Ann's Church, a notable landmark alongside Highway 97, stands on its original site near the ranch house. The oldest Catholic Church in the B.C. Interior, it was built in 1889 and is still in excellent repair.

With the junction of Highway 97 and Westside Road as km 0.0, head south past the Head-of-the-Lake Indian Village. The

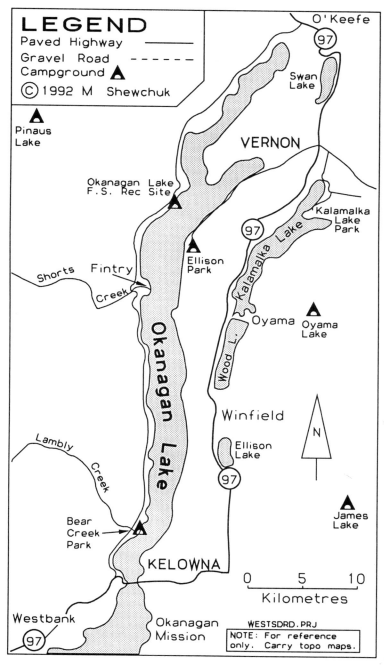

LEGEND
Paved Highway ————
Gravel Road - - - - -
Campground ▲
ⓒ 1992 M Shewchuk

Map 22: Westside Road.

dry hillsides alongside the road can appear to be quite barren in late summer, but in April and May they are mass of colour as wide variety of wildflowers compete for the spring rains.

The dry climate has also attracted a growing number of hobby farms, retirement communities and beach resorts. While lake access is limited, there are some excellent views, particularly near km 25. Be careful when you pull off the narrow road to enjoy the view.

F intry Delta Road, near km 35, marks the access to the mouth of Shorts Creek and one of the oldest communities on the west side of the lake. Captain T.D. Shorts, the first settler on the delta, was co-owner and master of the first powered freighter to ply Okanagan Lake. In partnership with Thomas Greenhow, Thomas Dolman Shorts launched the *Mary Victoria Greenhow* on the 21st of April, 1886. Unfortunately, the coal-oil burning two horsepower engine was much too small for the 32-foot-long ship and the maiden voyage to Penticton was considered by the owners, in retrospect, as a comedy of errors that cleaned out the valley's supply of lamp coal-oil.

T.D. Shorts later retired to Hope, B.C. where he died in 1921 at the age of 83. After Shorts, the delta land was owned, in succession, by The Honorable John Scott Montague, Viscount Ennismore, Sir John Poynder Dickson and The Honorable James Dunsmuir.

According to David Falconer, "Capt. J.C. Dun-Waters arrived in the Okanagan in 1909 and purchased the first parcel of land that was later to grow into Fintry Estate from a Major Audain. Dun-Waters named his new property after Fintry, Stirlingshire, Scotland, where he grew up on his family's estate...

"Originally, the growing of the finest Okanagan apples possible was Dun-Waters' chief interest. One hundred acres was planted to apples alone, and an extensive web of irrigation fluming was installed. The two suspension bridges [across Shorts Creek] were built in that pre-war period to support the wooden irrigation pipe."

J.C. Dun-Waters, who became known as the Laird of Fintry" was, according to Art Bailey, a bit of an eccentric. "When the passenger sternwheeler came into Fintry Landing he would often ask people what their religion was, and if it was to his liking, they received a bottle of his own scotch and were asked to join him ashore. Others were refused entry."

Arthur W. Bailey arrived in the Okanagan Valley in 1961, with the intention of developing Fintry into a California-style resort community. He concedes that he was "a little bit premature," but he did build a hotel complex at Fintry Estates. As part of his efforts, Bailey also built the sternwheeler, *Fintry Queen*, to carry clients to his resort before the paving of Westside Road was completed. Arthur Bailey sold out in 1981. The new buyers planned a major development, but the recession of the early '80s forced them into bankruptcy. According to Bailey, current owner Ken Johnstone has approvals for a major new resort.

Lake Okanagan Resort, near km 50, is a first-class facility that is attracting attention—and guests—world-wide. If you decide not to stop at the resort, you can pull over at an excellent viewpoint near km 54 or detour down to Okanagan Lake at Traders Cove Marine Park near km 60. The park entrance is opposite Bear Road (a.k.a Bear Lake Road) and if you're looking for a little more excitement, you could follow Bear Road southwest into the high country and join the Okanagan Connector just west of the summit.(See page 63 for details.)

Bear Creek Provincial Park, near km 61, is also well worth a stop. (See page 45.) The campground, beaches and canyon trails are all part of one of the more recent additions to British Columbia's park system. As you continue south from Bear Creek Provincial Park, watch the lakeshore nearer Westside for remnants of the docks that once served the Okanagan Lake ferry, prior to construction of the floating bridge. The junction of Westside Road and Highway 97 (km 68), a few minutes southwest of downtown Kelowna, is the southern terminal of this scenic backroad.

Do you cross the floating bridge to Kelowna or head to Westbank and points south? The decision is yours.

• • •

Additional Information Sources:

B.C. Parks
P.O. Box 399,
Summerland, B.C. V0H 1Z0

Lake Okanagan Resort
P.O. Box 1321,
Kelowna, B.C. V1Y 7V8
Tel: (604) 769-3511

Vernon Tourism
P.O. Box 520,
6326 Highway 97 North,
Vernon, B.C. V1T 6M4
Tel: (604) 542-1415

• • •

Fig. 40: Fairy Slipper (Calypso bulbosa) in the forest.

Mabel Lake Road (East Side)

Statistics	For map, see page 155.
Distance:	109 km, Lumby to Three Valley.
Travel Time:	Four to five hours minimum.
Elev. gain:	Minimal (High point approx. 550 metres).
Condition:	Part paved, some rough gravel sections.
Season:	North portion summer road only.
Topo Maps:	Sugar Lake, B.C. 82 L/SE (1:100,000).
	Revelstoke, B.C. 82 L/NE (1:100,000).
Forest Maps:	Salmon Arm and Area.
Communities:	Lumby, Enderby and Three Valley.

Lumby to Three Valley via Mabel Lake

The Mabel Lake area has held a special attraction to me ever since I had the opportunity to fly low over the area a decade ago. The long, narrow lake looked particularly inviting, partly because of its beauty but most importantly because of its apparent isolation. Time often has a way of passing without allowing dreams to be followed, but my wife and I decided to make time to follow our dream of exploring the area. Topographic maps presented conflicting information and our usually-reliable sources of rumors weren't much better. Except for information about frequent wash-outs near Wap Lake and a beautiful waterfall on Cascade Creek, we were on our own.

After much soul-searching, we decided that south to north seemed to be a good way to explore this backroad. Then if we were forced to turn back at Wap Lake, we would have at least seen the Mabel Lake area. The result was that on a mid-summer afternoon, the four-way stop light at the corner of Highway 6 (Vernon Street) and

Shuswap Avenue in Lumby became kilometre 0.0 for a sheaf of notes and a most interesting backroad adventure.

As we followed Shuswap Avenue north, the Trinity Valley Road, at km 4.9, became the first point of possible diversion. This road to the left leaves White Valley and follows Vance Creek and Trinity Creek northwest through Trinity Valley to Ashton Creek and on to Enderby, providing a scenic shortcut to the heart of the south Shuswap area. The road to Mabel Lake continues east down Bessette Creek to Shuswap Falls, passing through bottomland rich with hay, corn and livestock. Rollings Road, at km 11.5, provides an alternate route back to Highway 6 via Rawlings Lake.

The road on the east side of the Shuswap River, starting at the bridge, km 16.4, provides access to the rich land along the valley bottom on this southernmost loop of the Shuswap. The river rises in the heart of the rugged Monashee Mountains, north of Sugar Lake, before looping south to Cherryville. Dams at Brenda Falls at the foot of Sugar Lake and here at Shuswap Falls, near km 16.8, harness the flow of the river to generate electricity. Here at Wilsey Dam, B.C. Hydro has created a recreation area with a parking lot, biffies and trails to the falls and canyon. Paddlers on the river use the wide trails to portage the falls and rapids.

The road swings above the canyon at the foot of Shuswap Falls and doesn't return to river level for about six kilometres. Then it follows the river downstream toward Mabel Lake, reaching the beginning of a forestry road at km 27.9. An opening in the timber provides the first glimpse of the south end of Mabel Lake at km 34.8. A trail to the water's edge provides access to launch a cartop boat and fish the area around the river outlet. In the mid-1970s, the landowner attempted to sell much of the land near here to the government for use in Mabel Lake Park. The offer was declined, however, because of the swampy land and because park management saw no need to expand the park.

Mabel Lake Provincial Park, at km 37.9, proved to be a welcome sight as the summer afternoon wore on. Despite the season, there was still a choice of sites and we camped a stone's throw from the beach and playground. The beach delayed supper somewhat, but when everything was cleaned up, I settled down to read *Grassroots of Lumby: 1877-1927*, acquired earlier at the Lumby information centre. From it, I learned that the surrounding land first belonged to Reginald Sadler, a young Englishman who came to Canada at the turn of the century. T.A. Norris, Lumby's first school teacher later bought the lakeshore property and lived here for some time before selling it in the

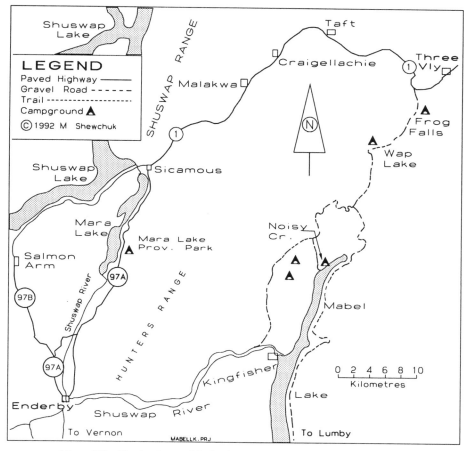

Map 23: Enderby -- Mabel Lake -- Three Valley Area.

1930s to satisfy a debt. Will Shields, who spent much of his life as a store keeper in Lumby, and Henry Sigalet, a pioneer lumberman, bought the property, building comfortable summer homes near the lake.

Born in Ontario in 1884, Shields came to Lumby about 1910 and retired to the Vernon area in 1956. Henry Sigalet was born in Alberta in 1899 and came to the Okanagan Valley two years later. In the midst of the depression, Henry Sigalet built a lumber mill in nearby Squaw Valley, and in 1940 he opened a mill in Lumby. Both Shields and Sigalet died in 1972, not long after completing negotiations on the sale of the property for the Mabel Lake Park site.

The majority of park development work took place during the period of 1978-80, but additions to the playground and a water system have been made more recently. The 85-unit campground has an attractive 2100 metre long shoreline with an excellent beach. Hemlock, red cedar and birch shade the property, indicative of the cooler, wetter climate compared to the dry Okanagan Valley. A guide to the Rainforest Interpretive Trail is also available at the park.

The gravel road winds along the mountainside well above the lake as it continues north of the park. Logging roads offer the occasional diversion as do roaring creeks. A small sign on a bend in the road near km 43.0 signals the beginning of the trail into Cascade Falls. The falls lives up to its name and it resembles an ever broadening veil as it tumbles down the steep rocky slope. The 300-metre trail to the foot of the waterfall will require some caution but otherwise is not difficult. A tripod and wide-angle lens will help when photographing the falls and a close-up lens will prove useful for the many fungi, berries and wildflowers along the trail.

As we continued northward along the main road, Torrent Creek, a boulder-strewn waterway at km 50.9 marked our first return to Mabel Lake since leaving the provincial park. The occasional logging road climbs away from the main track, but otherwise Mabel Lake Road follows the timbered benches until it swings east to avoid the narrow canyon of Tsiuis Creek as it descends to the creek crossing at km 61.3. If Wap Lake and Three Valley is your destination, keep left at all the major junctions.

The road climbs high above the lake, then begins to descend and you may catch a brief glimpse of the north end of Mabel Lake through the trees at km 80.0. A short distance beyond the end of the lake, the road winds through recent logging areas. Some maps suggest that the old road around the north end of the lake once crossed Wap River near here, but what could have been this link now looked unused and impassable.

From the north end of Mabel Lake to the Wap River crossing at km 89.0, the road varies from good gravel to somewhat lumpy backroad conditions. The creek crossings show signs of the terrific force of torrential rains that can occur almost any time of the year. Portions of the road in this area are narrow and rough, but should pose little difficulty for most two-wheel-drive vehicles. The forest roads that veer east off the main road often appear better and more used, but this can be deceiving—a point brought home when one suddenly ends up at a dead-end in a log landing.

The junction near km 90, a short distance north of the Wap River bridge, is the first left turn that is ignored in the relentless search for Three Valley Gap. The road to the left (west) climbs steadily to a high

Fig. 41: Cascade Falls, east of Mabel Lake.

valley paralleling the west side of Mabel Lake and then continues south to the Shuswap River outflow of Mabel Lake. Portions of this route parallel the 500,000 volt power lines linking the Revelstoke hydro-electric plant with a major B.C. Hydro substation at Ashton Creek, near Enderby.

The road straight ahead again crosses the Wap River at km 93 after traversing a few sandy sections. Recent roadwork and logging debris suggest that logging has been active for several years. The road passes under the 500 kilovolt power line a short distance beyond the bridge and swings left through the timber.

It may not be apparent at first, but the gravel road and the Wap Lake West Recreation Site, at km 97, sit on what was once a railway bed. A logging railway, built near the turn of the century, wound into the heart of this valley from the Canadian Pacific Railway mainline at Three Valley Lake.

Wap lake is unusual in that the railway bed allows good casting from the shoreline as well as providing several places to launch a canoe or cartop boat. Camping sites are limited to a few at the rec site and a few other wide spots in the road. While I tried my hand at casting from the shore, the rest of the motley crew picked huckleberries and blueberries to make a campfire desert. A tasty frying-pan upside-down cake compensated for my usual lack of trout for the same frying pan.

Beyond Wap Lake, the backroad skirts the marshes and the river, bouncing over several rough sections that could be difficult in wet weather. New culverts in two locations indicated that my information sources may have been right—the road was washed out between the lake and the bridge at km 104.5. At the time of our passage, this steel-framed bridge across the Wap River was in excellent repair, but a nearby heap of logs and decaying planks indicated that it was not always so. A four-wheel-drive vehicle with good clearance could ford the river in low water, but a car might find the boulders a bit lumpy.

An old sign in a tree just north of the bridge points to an overgrown trail upstream to Frog Falls. Huge cedar stumps stand like guards at the hidden trail entrance. However, a few hundred metres beyond the bridge, a side road leads into an excellent Forest Service Rec Site and a wider trail to the crest of the falls.

The trail to the falls passes one of the largest private hydroelectric plants in B.C., buried in the mountain side. Faced with an estimated $450,000 tab from B.C. Hydro to run lines from Revelstoke or Malakwa to his resort at Three Valley, Gordon Bell set out to build his own power plant using the 100 foot head developed at Frog Falls. After obtaining the necessary permits from seven different bureaucracies, Bell went ahead with construction.

The Three Valley system is unusual in two ways. First, it uses water pumps operating as turbines to drive the electric generator instead of the usual more expensive specially-designed turbines. And secondly, it is a constant load system, using an electronically controlled load distribution system to maintain a steady AC supply while heating and lighting the complete resort. Bell's system cost almost 75 per cent of what Hydro would have charged, but his real saving is in the elimination of an enormous monthly energy bill.

Beyond the Frog Falls recreation site the much-improved road begins a steady descent to Three Valley Lake, following South Pass Creek and the old logging railway bed much of the way. Labeled the "Three Valley-Mabel Lake Forest Service Road" at the north end, km 109.0, this backroad joins Highway 1 near the west end of Three Valley Lake, approximately 21 kilometres west of Revelstoke.

● ● ●

Additional Information Sources

B.C. Parks
Okanagan District,
P.O. Box 399,
Summerland, B.C. V0H 1Z0

Gordon Bell,
Three Valley Gap Motor Inn,

Highway 1, Box 860,
Revelstoke, B.C. V0E 2S0
Tel: (604) 837-2109

Ministry of Forests,
Salmon Arm, B.C.
Tel: (604) 832-7153

● ● ●

Fig. 42: Picking huckelberries near Wap Lake.

The Mabel Lake Shortcut

Statistics	For map, see page 155.
Distance:	Approx. 90 km, Three Valley Lake to Enderby.
Travel Time:	Two to four hours.
Condition:	Some rough gravel, may be closed in winter.
Season:	July through October.
Topo Maps:	Shuswap Lake, B.C. 82 L/NW (1:100,000).
	Revelstoke, B.C. 82 L/NE (1:100,000).
Forest Maps:	Salmon Arm and Area.
Communities:	Revelstoke, Sicamous and Enderby.

Three Valley to Enderby via Mabel Lake.

If you are looking for an excuse to get off the pavement while on your way from the Rockies to the Okanagan, this British Columbia backcountry road is a few kilometres shorter than the regular route via Sicamous. But as is the case with most backroad shortcuts, the Mabel Lake Shortcut will probably take you twice as long as it would if you stuck to Highway 1 and Highway 97A.

There are, however, two major reasons to make a mid-summer meander through the heart of the Monashee Mountains. The first reason is to get away from the hell-bent-for-destruction crowds that seem to be intent on turning the Trans-Canada Highway into a training ground for crash-test dummies. The second reason is actually much more positive than negative—unless you just happen to be a fish—and it is the relatively easy access to quiet recreation sites on Wap Lake, Mabel Lake and several other off-the-road lakes.

Take note of my mention of mid-summer. The north end of this route passes through the heart of the Monashee rain forest and ease of access depends on logging activity and the prerequisite road maintenance.

Washouts and late-season snow drifts are common on the section be-tween Three Valley Lake and Wap Lake, so a full fuel tank, a shovel and lots of time are definite requirements before heading south. These items, plus a chainsaw or a good swede saw and an axe should be part of any backroad explorer's kit regardless of where he or she is heading.

The Mabel Lake Shortcut hasn't gone unnoticed by others. There were rumors more than a decade ago that the government was considering routing a brand-new four-lane highway through here in a direct link from Revelstoke to the Okanagan Valley and then the Coast via the Okanagan/Coquihalla Connector. The arguments then—and now—are that this route, if continued down the west side of Okanagan Lake, would bypass most of the congestion and development of the Shuswap, Okanagan and Thompson valleys. I have no idea if this option is still being considered and I don't intend to ask anyone. It's much more fun to speculate based on true ignorance than on inside knowl-edge.

We've made the trip several times during the past half-dozen years. The first was in mid-August, 1986, and washouts and questionable bridges were the rule, rather than exception. By August, 1988, a rotting bridge across the Wap River had been replaced by a steel structure and most of the washouts had been re-routed or rebuilt with larger culverts. In late July, 1991, the road, though narrow and rough in spots, was easily passable by cars or light trucks with fair clearance. Logging was active south of Wap Lake and logging trucks could be expected at any time. Although logging activity changes from year to year, it is prob-ably safest to travel this route on weekends or evenings. Better yet, contact the Forest Service office at Salmon Arm (832-7153) for up-to-date information.

For the purpose of this backroad trip, kilometre "0" is the junction of the Trans-Canada Highway and Wap-Mabel Road, 20 kilo-metres west of Revelstoke near the west end of Three Valley Lake. A signpost a short distance off the highway also marked it as the "Three Valley-Mabel Lake Forest Service Road". The grade is easy here, with smooth wide corners that hint that this is not your average logging road. A bridge at km 1.3 that looks remarkably like a railway bridge confirms the suspicion that other methods of transportation may have been used here before rubber-tired vehicles became king of the backroad.

David Stewart, himself a semi-retired king of the backroads, has a plausible explanation in *Okanagan Backroads Volume 2,* published by Saltaire in 1975 and long out of print:

"The valley of the Wap has an interesting past," writes Dave Stewart. "Around the turn of the century, an English firm with headquarters in London built a logging railroad from Three Valley, on the CP main line, in past Wap Lake. Until two or three decades ago, traces of the old railway could be seen, along with a steam donkey engine and the big old stumps left by the loggers of that far-away time. In 1948 I stumbled on several racks of steel rails not far west of Wap Lake (we called it Frog Lake those days). Presumably this steel is still hidden in the dense underbrush: the logging railway it had been intended to extend having disappeared over the intervening four decades."

Gordon Bell, owner of the Three Valley Gap Motor Inn at the east end of Three Valley Lake, had the good fortune of meeting one of the descendants of the original operators. According to his information, the logging railway once extended as far south as Mabel Lake, with spur lines up many of the side valleys. The company operated one of the largest sawmills in western Canada at the west end of Three Valley Lake with, says Gordon, three planers, a post office and a hotel. The Bell House hotel (no relation) was later dismantled and moved to the top of Mount Revelstoke where it became the Mount Revelstoke Chalet until Parks Canada tore it down around 1970.

Giant stumps, some with the spring-board notches still clearly visible, surround the Frog Falls F.S. Rec Site at km 4.3. Nearby Wap River starts in the southeast on the slopes of Mount Begbie, and after a northward rush, swings south here as it twists and tumbles down to Mabel Lake. A wide trail leads from the Rec Site to the crest of the 25 metre (80 foot) two-step Frog Falls.

The trail to the falls passes, buried in the mountain side, what was, until recently, one of the largest private hydroelectric plants in B.C. Faced with an estimated $450,000 tab from B.C. Hydro to run lines from Revelstoke or Malakwa to his resort at Three Valley Gap, Gordon Bell set out to build his own power plant using the 100 foot head developed at Frog Falls and two additional run-of-the river dams farther upstream. After obtaining the necessary permits from seven different bureaucracies, Bell went ahead with construction.

The Three Valley Gap system is unusual in two ways. First, it uses water pumps operating as turbines to drive the 150,000 watt electric generator instead of the more expensive specially-designed turbines. And secondly, it is a constant load system, using an electronically controlled load distribution system to maintain a steady AC supply while heating and lighting the complete resort. Bell's system cost almost what Hydro would have charged, but his real saving is in the elimination of an enormous monthly energy bill.

The road south of the Rec Site and the Wap River bridge follows the old rail bed near the valley floor. Several side roads lead to the left into the high country and some maps hint that there may be a route to Sugar Lake through here, but I haven't yet confirmed that rumor. Water lily marshes near km 10.7 are the first hint of Wap Lake, but it is almost two kilometres farther along the old rail bed before you reach the small Forest Service Rec Site at the west end of the lake.

South of the lake, the road swings away from the river for several kilometres, skirting a knoll before crossing under a 500,000 volt power line near km 16 and again crossing the river half a kilometre farther along. The B.C. Hydro power line links the Revelstoke hydro plant with the rest of the system at the Ashton Creek substation near Enderby.

A junction near km 19.5 marks the beginning of a climb away from the valley floor. On our last trip through, a small sign labeled "Enderby Eventually" signaled the start of the Kingfisher Forest Service Road. The road to the right leads to Enderby, while the road to the left again crosses Wap River, and with a little luck and good planning could take you all the way to Lumby.

Kingfisher F.S. Road climbs steadily, reaching an elevation of about 850 metres (2800 feet) before it crosses into the Noisy Creek drainage. Side roads lead into several old log cuts (and a few newer ones) where wild blueberries, raspberries, huckleberries and moose are plentiful. The roadside markers begin a countdown as you continue south. Another junction just south of the 21K marker (km 36 from Three Valley) marks the route down to Noisy Creek F.S. Rec Site at Mabel Lake. Its a five kilometre drive down to the lake, but the large Rec Site and excellent beach is well worth the trip. In fact, the site is actually two quite different campgrounds split by Noisy Creek and its delta. The south campground looks down the lake with a few waterfront campsites and a larger number sheltered in the trees. The campground north of the delta gets the morning sun and could be better protected in the case of a storm. Although the road was somewhat rough, it was passable to truck campers and a variety of other vehicles in the summer of '91. According to some of the campers we talked to, this has been a popular site for at least 30 years. Firewood is usually in short supply, so plan on collecting wood from the old logged areas on your way down.

Beyond the Noisy Creek junction, Kingfisher Road crosses into the Danforth Creek drainage. Rough side roads lead west into Mount Mara and the Hunters Range and east into Stony, Holiday and Noreen lakes.

Fig. 43: Mabel Lake, from Noisy Creek recreation site.

Then the backroad parallels the Kingfisher Creek valley before making a long, winding descent to Mabel Lake Road and the Shuswap River.

Kingfisher, at the western outlet of Mabel Lake, is a small resort community that comes alive during the summer. Located at the end of the pavement 37 km east of Enderby and about five kilometres east of the junction with the Kingfisher F.S. Road, it may be your last chance for supplies if you are following the Wap Lake route north.

The route west to Enderby passes through a fine pastoral valley with several access points to the Shuswap River. Canoeists favor the river, and except for the Skookumchuck Rapids near the outlet of Mabel Lake, it is considered "rather tranquil and a large breeding ground for Canada Geese." A junction near the Ashton Creek General Store, 10 km east of Enderby, presents another backroad detour south through the Trinity Valley to Lumby. But if Enderby and Highway 97A is your present destination, continue west through the broad Shuswap River Valley and you'll soon be back at civilization.

•••

Additional Information Sources:

B.C. Parks
Okanagan District,
P.O. Box 399,
Summerland, B.C. V0H 1Z0

Gordon Bell,
Three Valley Gap Motor Inn,

Highway 1, Box 860,
Revelstoke, B.C. V0E 2S0
Tel: (604) 837-2109

Ministry of Forests,
Salmon Arm.

•••

Bibliography and Sources
Selected Bibliography

Barlee, N.L. *Gold Creeks and Ghost Towns.* Hancock House Publishers Ltd., Surrey, B.C. Third edition, second printing 1988.

Burbridge, Joan. *Wildflowers of the Southern Interior of British Columbia and adjacent parts of Washington, Idaho and Montana.* University of British Columbia Press, Vancouver, B.C. 1989.

Falk, Les. *Hiking Trails in the Okanagan.* Mosaic Enterprises Limited, Kelowna, B.C. 1982.

Hatton, William J. *Bridesville Country: A Brief History.* Oliver Printing, Oliver, B.C. 1981.

Hill, Beth. *Exploring the Kettle Valley Railway.* Polestar Press, Winlaw, B.C. 1989.

Lyons, C.P. *Trees, Shrubs and Flowers to know in British Columbia.* Toronto, ON. 1952.

McLean, Stan. *The History of the O'Keefe Ranch.* Stan McLean, Vernon, B.C. 1984.

Peachland Memories, Volume One. Published by the Peachland Historical Society, Box 244, Peachland, B.C., V0H 1X0 1983.

Peachland Memories, Volume Two. Published by the Peachland Historical Society, Box 244, Peachland, B.C., V0H 1X0 1983.

Peachey, Gordon. *The Okanagan.* Gordon Peachey, Kelowna, B.C. 1984.

Read, Stanley E. *A Place Called Pennask.* Mitchell Press, Vancouver, B.C. 1977.

Sanford, Barrie. *McCulloch's Wonder —The Story of the Kettle Valley Railway—* Whitecap Books, North Vancouver, B.C. 1977.

Shewchuk, Murphy O. *Backroads Explorer Vol. 2 Similkameen & South Okanagan.* Hancock House Publishers Ltd. Surrey, B.C. 1988.

Shewchuk, Murphy O. *Coquihalla Country: An Outdoor Recreation Guide.* Sonotek Publishing Ltd. Merritt, B.C. 1990 (revised 1991).

Shewchuk, Murphy O. *Exploring the Nicola Valley.* Douglas & McIntyre, Vancouver, B.C. 1981.

Shewchuk, Murphy O. *Fur, Gold & Opals.* Hancock House Publishers Ltd. Surrey, B.C. 1975.

Surtees,Ursula. *Kelowna: The Orchard City. An Illustrated History.* (includes *Partners in Progress* by Mark Zuehlke). Windsor Publications, Ltd. 1989.

Woolliams, Nina G. *Cattle Ranch: The Story of the Douglas Lake Cattle Company.* Douglas & McIntyre, Vancouver, B.C. 1979.

Maps

Topographic Maps

(1:50,000):
Kelowna, B.C. 82 E/14
Peachland, B.C. 82 E/13
Summerland, B.C. 82 E/12

(1:100,000):
Grand Forks, B.C. 82 E/SE
Kelowna, B.C. 82 E/NW
Penticton, B.C. 82E/SW

Princeton, B.C. 92H/SE
Revelstoke, B.C. 82 L/NE
Sugar Lake, B.C. 82 L/SE
Tulameen, B.C. 92 H/NE
Vernon, B.C. 82 L/SW

Forest Service Maps
Merritt and Area
Penticton and Area
Salmon Arm and Area
Vernon and Area

Addresses

BC Parks,
West Kootenay District,
4750 Hwy 3A, RR #3,
Nelson, B.C. V1L 5P6
Tel: (604) 825-4421

BC Parks, Okanagan District,
P.O. Box 399,
Summerland, B.C. V0H 1Z0
Tel: (604) 494-0321

Crystal Mountain,
P.O. Box 97,
Westbank, B.C. V0H 2A0
Tel: (604) 768-5189

Ecological Reserves Program,
Ministry of Parks
Parliament Buildings,
Victoria, B.C. V8V 1X4

Headwaters Fishing Camp,
Box 350, Peachland, B.C.
V0H 1X0
Tel: (604) 767-2400

Kelowna Chamber of Commerce
544 Harvey Avenue,
Kelowna, B.C. V1Y 6C9
Tel: (604) 861-1515

Ministry of Forests
1634 Carmi Ave.
Penticton, B.C. V2A 6Z1
Tel: (604) 492-8721

Mount Baldy Ski Area,
c/o Borderline Ski Club,
P.O. Box 1528,
Oliver, B.C. V0H 1T0
Tel: (604) 498-2262

North Okanagan Cross Country
Ski Club,
P.O. Box 1543,
Vernon, B.C. V1T 8C2

Okanagan Similkameen Parks
Society,
Box 787,
Summerland, B.C. V0H 1Z0

Oliver and District Chamber of
Commerce,
P.O. Box 460,
Oliver, B.C. V0H 1T0

Penticton Chamber of
Commerce,
210 Main Street,
Penticton, B.C. V2A 5B2
Tel: (604) 492-4103

Silver Star Mountain Resort,
P.O. Box 2,
Silver Star Mountain, B.C.
V0E 1G0
Tel: (604) 542-0224

Summerland Chamber of
Commerce,
Box 1075, Highway 97,
Summerland, B.C. V0H 1Z0
Tel: (604) 494-2686

Telemark Cross Country Ski
Club,
P.O. Box 747,
Westbank, B.C. V0H 2A0

Vernon Tourism,
6326 Highway 97 North,
Vernon, B.C. V1T 6M4
Tel: (604) 542-1415

!

350th Avenue, 108, 111

A

Adra Tunnel, 27, 31
Aeneas Lake, 84
Allison Creek Valley, 82
Allison Trail, 52
Anarchist Mountain, 114, 116
Apex Alpine Ski Resort, 83, 87
Apex Mountain, 70, 87-88
Ashnola River, 92
Ashton Creek, 154, 158, 164, 166

B

Bailey, Arthur, 151
Baker Lake, 21
Bald Range Road, 80
Barlee, N.L., 35, 116
bass, 127
Beaconsfield Mountain, 87
Bear Creek, 47
Bear Creek Park, 13, 16, 45, 47,
58, 68, 147, 152
Bear Creek Ranch, 45
Bear Road, 58, 63, 66, 68
Beaverdell, 35, 37
Belfort Creek, 82
Bell, Gordon, 158, 163
Bellevue Creek, 30
Benvoulin Road, 44
Bertram Creek Regional Park, 19, 23
Bessette Creek, 154
Big Teepee, 104
Big White Ski Resort, 35, 41, 124
biking, mountain, 27, 31, 138
Black Sage Road, 132
Blind Creek, 102
Boicy, Jack, 123
Borderline Ski Club, 114
Boulder Trail, 23
Boyce, Benjamin De Furlong, 15

Brenda Falls, 154
Brenda Lake, 58
Brenda Mine Road, 58, 62
Bridesville, 111, 116, 120
Brink, Dr. Vernon, 96
Buchan Bay, 24
burbot, 137
Burbridge, Joan, 18, 167
Burnell (Sawmill) Lake, 102

C

cactus, prickly-pear, 24, 47, 72,
102, 126
Cahill Creek, 89
Cameo Lake, 67
Camp McKinney, 106, 108, 116, 120
Canadian Pacific Railway, 36
Cariboo, 107
Cariboo-Amelia Claim, 116
Carmi, 36, 38
carp, 137
Cascade Creek, 153
Cascade Falls, 156
Cascade Mountains, 92, 102
Casorso Road, 44
Cathedral Lakes Lodge, 91, 94
Cathedral Lakes Resort Ltd., 98
Cathedral Mountain, 94, 96
Cathedral Park, 70, 91-92, 98
Cawston, 99
Cedar Creek Estate Winery, 23
Chain Lake, 82
Cherryville, 154
Christian Valley, 37-38
Chute Creek, 25
Chute Lake, 30-32, 76
Chute Lake Resort, 30-32
Chute Lake Road, 13, 23, 25, 30-32
Clark, Herb, 94, 98
Clark, L.A., 84
Coalmont, 82
Coates, Jack, 120, 124
Coldstream, 139

Coldstream Orchards, 84
Columbia River, 107
Commando Bay, 24
Conkle Lake, 119-120, 123
Conkle Lake Loop, 119
Conkle Lake Park, 38, 118-119, 123-124
Coquihalla Canyon, 36
Coquihalla Connector, 162
Cosens Bay, 140
Coulthard, John, 100
Cranbrook, 125
Crawford Lake, 30
Crescent Lake, 61
Crown Zellerbach Canada Limited, 45
Crowsnest Route, 82
Crystal Mountain, 50, 67

D

Danforth Creek, 164
Darke Lake, 80
Devil's Fenceposts, 98
Divide Lake, 21, 23, 25-26
Dole, James D., 64
Dominion Radio Astrophysical Observatory, 110
Douglas Lake, 58
Ducks Unlimited, 130
Dun-Waters, J.C., 151

E

Echo Lake Park, 138
Echo Lake Resort, 138
Elinor Lake F.S. Road, 31-32
Ellis Street, 15
Ellis, Tom, 52
Ellison Park, 135
Enderby, 67, 154, 158, 164, 166
Evans, Tom, 120

F

Fairview, 108-109
Fairview Camp, 102, 104
Fairview Hotel, 104
Fairview Road, 84, 99, 104, 106, 108-109
Falk, Les, 167
Farleigh Lake, 84
Farrell, Ron, 55, 61
Father Pandosy, 44
Fintry Delta Road, 151

Fintry Estate, 151
Fish Lake, 79
Fleet, Tom, 98
Fort Okanogan, 107
Fort St. James, 107
Frog Falls, 158, 163
Frog Falls F.S. Rec Site, 158, 163

G

Gehringer, Helmut, 94, 98
Gehringer, Karl, 94, 98
Gemmill Lake Road, 25
Giant Cleft, 98
Giant's Head Mountain, 75
Giant's Head Road, 75
Gibbard, Bob, 32
Gillard Creek Road, 27, 29
Glacier Lake, 94, 96
Glenfir, 32
Glenrosa Road, 50
gold, 47, 90, 102, 104, 109, 111
Golden Gate Hotel, 104
Goode's Basin Trail, 24
Goode's Creek Canyon, 21
Gorman's Mill, 52
Greata Creek, 62
Green Lake, 109
Green Lake Road, 109
Green Mountain House, 84, 87
Green Mountain Road, 83-84, 87
Greenhow, Thomas, 148, 151

H

Halloween Trees, 114
Hardy Falls Park, 13, 51
Hardy Street, 51
Hardy, Harry, 52
Hatheume Lake, 58, 66
Hatton, Bill, 114
Haynes Ecological Reserve, 130
Haynes Lake, 41
Haynes Point Park, 125-126
Haynes, John Carmichael, 125
Headwaters Fishing Camp, 55, 61
Headwaters Lakes, 56, 60, 82
Hedley, 83, 89
Hedley Mascot, 89
Hedley-Nickel Plate F.S. Road, 87
Highland Bell Mine, 38
Highway 3, 33, 39, 99, 116, 120
Highway 33, 33, 36, 39, 41, 120, 123
Highway 3A, 99, 110

Highway 5A, 82
Highway 97, 32-33, 41, 45, 51, 62, 79, 106, 110-111, 124, 147
Highway 97A, 161
Highway 97C, 56, 63
Holiday Lake, 164
Hudson's Bay Company, 107, 126
Hunters Range, 164
Hydraulic Creek, 42
Hydraulic Lake, 41

I

Idabel Lake, 41
Inkaneep Forest, 114
Inkaneep Indian Reserve, 113
Interior Plateau, 63
Iverson, Robert, 104

J

Jackpine F.S. Road, 67
Jackpine Lake, 67
Joe Rich Valley, 35
Johnstone Creek, 118, 120
Johnstone Creek Park, 118

K

K.L.O. Road, 44
Kalamalka Lake, 139, 141
Kalamalka Lake Park, 138-140
Kalamalka Road, 139
Kaleden, 110
Kamloops, 45
Kekuli Bay Park, 141
Kelly River, 124
Kelowna, 13, 15, 18, 23-24, 28, 30, 33, 36, 42, 45, 50, 58, 68, 71, 107, 147
Kelowna Centennial Museum, 16
Keremeos, 83-84, 92, 99-100, 110
Keremeos Creek, 100
Keremeos Grist Mill, 99-100
Kettle Forest, 114
Kettle River Museum, 39
Kettle River Park, 38
Kettle Valley, 118
Kettle Valley Railroad, 76
Kettle Valley Railway, 27, 30-32, 36, 42, 76, 79, 81
Kingfisher, 166
Kingfisher Creek, 166
Kingfisher F.S. Road, 164, 166
Klahanie, 94

Knox Mountain, 13, 15-16
Knox Mountain Park, 15
Knox, Arthur Booth, 15
kokanee, 47, 137

L

Lacoma Creek, 67
Lady Slipper Lake, 96
Lake of the Woods, 96
Lake Okanagan Resort, 152
Lakeshore Road, 13, 23, 30
Lambly Creek, 67
Lambly Lake, 67
Lambly, Charles, 67
Lambly, Robert, 52, 67
Lambly, Thomas, 67
Last Mountain, 50
Lebanon Lake, 30
Link Lake, 82
Little Fish Lake, 120
Little Loon Lake, 61
Little White Mountain, 30
Lowe Drive, 102
Lumby, 38, 138, 154-155, 164
Lyons, Ches, 92, 94

M

Mabel Lake, 153-154, 156, 158, 161, 163-164, 166
Mabel Lake Park, 138, 154-155
Mabel Lake Road, 156, 166
Mabel Lake Shortcut, 161-162
MacDonald Lake, 58
Madden Lake, 102
Mahoney Lake, 109
Marron Valley Road, 84
Martin, Frank, 120
McCulloch Road, 27, 41-42
McCulloch Station, 27, 36
McCulloch, Andrew, 36, 42, 82
McKeen, Jim, 94
McKinney Creek, 116
McKinney Road, 111, 113-114
McMillan Planetarium, 138
Metter, Fred, 31
Midway, 36, 39
Mission Creek, 35, 44
Mission Creek Park, 13, 44
Moffatt's Saloon, 104
Monashee Mountains, 153-154, 161
Monashee Pass, 38
Mount Baldy, 106, 111, 114

Mount Baldy Road, 111
Mount Begbie, 163
Mount Boucherie, 42
Mount Revelstoke, 163
Mountain Goat Trail, 25-26
Mt. Brent, 87
Mt. Hawthorne, 109
Mt. McKeen, 94

N

Naramata, 13, 25, 27-28, 30-32, 42, 76
Naramata Road, 25, 32
Nickel Plate Lake, 88-89
Nickel Plate Mine, 83-84, 89
Nickel Plate Mountain, 83
Nickel Plate Nordic Centre, 88
Nickel Plate Park, 88
Noisy Creek, 164
Noisy Creek F.S. Rec Site, 164
Noreen Lake, 164
Norman Lake, 21
Norris, T.A., 154
North Okanagan, 135

O

O'Keefe Ranch Museum, 133, 138, 147
Ogopogo, 47
Okanagan Centre, 15
Okanagan Connector, 63, 66, 68, 162
Okanagan desert, 111
Okanagan Falls, 41, 81, 110, 123-124
Okanagan Highlands, 111, 113
Okanagan Lake, 13, 21, 23, 32, 45, 56, 58, 66-67, 70-71, 74-76, 119, 137, 162
Okanagan Lake Park, 71, 74
Okanagan Mission, 13, 18, 23, 44, 107
Okanagan Mountain, 21, 23, 25, 76
Okanagan Mountain Park, 13, 21, 23, 25, 70, 74, 76
Okanagan Range, 92
Okanagan River, 70, 106, 111, 129-130
Okanagan Similkameen Parks Society, 123
Okanagan Valley, 35, 41, 45, 52, 62, 71, 76, 99, 102, 105, 109, 125, 155-156
Okanogan Valley, U.S.A., 125
Olalla, 87, 110
Old Hedley Road, 82
Oliver, 99, 102, 104, 106, 108-109, 111, 116, 120, 132
Orchard Museum, 16
Oregon, 102
Orofino Mountain, 99, 102
Oroville, Washington, 104
Osoyoos, 106, 116, 120, 125, 139
Osoyoos Lake, 70, 125, 130
Osprey Lake, 79, 82
Osprey Lakes Road, 79, 82
Otter Bay, 137
Otter Lake Park, 82

P

Pacific Fur Company, 107
Pacific rattlesnake, 24
Pandosy Mission, 44
Pandosy Street, 23, 28
Pandosy, Father, 107
Park Rill, 109
Peachland, 13, 51-52, 54-55, 62
Peachland Creek, 51, 60, 62
Peachland F.S. Road, 61-62
Peachland Historical Society, 167
Peachland Lake, 60
Pennask Creek, 58, 63
Pennask Lake, 58, 63-64
Pennask Lake Club, 66
Pennask Lake Recreation Area, 66
Pennask Mountain, 56, 62
Penticton, 24-25, 32, 36, 42, 52, 71, 76, 83, 106
Perrault, Ernest G., 94
Pinnacle Lake, 66
Powers Creek, 67
Prairie Valley Road, 75-76, 79
Price, Barrington, 100
Princeton, 52, 76, 82
Princeton-Summerland Road, 62, 79, 82
Provincial Park
  Apex Mountain, 88
  Bear Creek, 13, 16, 45, 58, 68, 147, 152
  Cathedral, 91-92, 98
  Conkle Lake, 38, 118-119, 123
  Echo Lake, 138
  Ellison, 135

Okanagan Country

Haynes Point, 125
Kalamalka Lake, 138-139
Kekuli Bay, 141
Kettle River, 38
Mabel Lake, 138, 154
Nickel Plate, 70
Okanagan Lake, 71, 74
Okanagan Mountain, 13, 21, 23, 74, 76
Pennask Lake, 66
Silver Star, 138, 145
Putnam Creek, 144
Pyramid Lake, 94, 96
Pyramid Mountain, 97

Q

Quilchena, 58
Quiniscoe Lake, 92, 94, 96

R

Rattlesnake Hill, 140
Rawlings Lake, 154
Raymer Road, 18
Read, Stanley E., 167
Reed, Gary, 31
Revelstoke, 158-159, 162
Rhone, 120, 123
Rice Creek, 116
Ripley Lake, 102
Ripperto, 120
Ripperto Creek, 124
Road 200, 124
Robinson Avenue, 32
Robinson, J.M., 52, 54
Rock Creek, 33, 39, 67, 116, 119-120, 125
rock ovens, 31-32
Rutland, 33, 41

S

Sadler, Reginald, 154
Salmon Arm, 162
Sand Point Drive, 113
Separation Lakes, 82
Shatford Road, 87
Sheep Rock, 87
Shewchuk, Murphy O., 176
Shields, Will, 155
Shingle Creek, 87
Shorts Creek, 151
Shorts, T.D., 151
Shuswap Falls, 154

Shuswap River, 154, 158, 166
Shuttleworth Canyon, 124
Sigalet, Henry, 155
silver, 83, 90, 102, 104
Silver Lake Camp, 62
Silver Star Mountain, 144
Silver Star Park, 138, 145
Similkameen River, 70, 92
Similkameen Valley, 90, 99-100, 102
Simpson, Stanley Merriam, 15
Skaha Lake, 32, 70, 76, 119
Ski Resort
  Apex Alpine, 83, 87
  Big White, 35, 41, 124
  Crystal Mountain, 50
  Mount Baldy, 111
  Silver Star, 144
skiing
  alpine, 35, 50, 111, 138
  Nordic, 31, 35, 50, 111, 138
Skookumchuck Rapids, 166
Smethurst Road, 31-32
Smokey the Bear, 98
Solco Lake, 124
Sonoran Desert, 24, 113
South Okanagan, 69
South Okanagan Land Co., 124
South Pass Creek, 159
Sovereign Lake, 145
Spallumcheen, 52, 147
Spences Bridge, 81
Springfield Road, 44
Squaw Valley, 155
St. Ann's Church (Hedley), 90
St. Ann's Church (O'Keefe), 148
Stemwinder Mine, 104
Stewart, David, 162
Stone City, 98
Stony Lake, 164
Stuart, David, 107
Sugar Lake, 154
Sullivan, 120
Sumac Ridge, 79
Summerland, 62, 71, 75-76, 79, 82
Summerland Agricultural Research Station, 76
Summerland Irrigation District, 61
Sunset Lake, 58
Sunset Lake Road, 58, 61
Sunset Main Road, 56, 58, 63
Sutherland Park, 16